Technique of

Hydrotherapy

and Swedish Massage

GEORGE KNAPP ABBOTT, M. D.

Hydrotherapy for Students and Prac-
f Medicine," "Elements of Hy-
herapy for Nurses"

eturned on or
ned below

Technique of Hydrotherapy

The Treatment of Disease by the Use of Water

The beneficial results are mainly derived from the application of heat or cold supplemented by mechanical effects rather than from the water itself.

CLASSIFICATION OF PROCEDURES

BECAUSE of similarity in technique and for convenience of description, the procedures of hydrotherapy have been classified under the following thirteen heads:

1. **Local Applications of Heat.** These include localized applications of heat to such areas as the abdomen, the spine, the chest, or a joint. Examples: the fomentation, hot-water bottle, radiant heat.

2. **Local Applications of Cold.** These are circumscribed applications of cold to such areas as those mentioned above. Examples: ice bag, cold-water coil.

3. **Heating Compresses.** A heating compress is a local application of moist heat made by applying next to the skin a cloth wrung from cold water, and so covered with flannel or an impervious covering as to cause an accumulation of body heat. Examples: moist chest pack, moist abdominal girdle, heating compress to throat.

4. **Poultices.** A poultice is an application of moist heat made by means of a semisolid mixture of various substances, and applied to the body while hot. Examples: flaxseed, clay and glycerin, charcoal.

5. **Tonic Frictions.** A tonic friction is an application of cold water so combined with fric-

tion as to produce stimulating or tonic effects. Examples: cold mitten friction, wet sheet rub.

6. Sponging. Sponging or ablution consists in the application of a liquid by means of a sponge, a cloth, or the bare hand, in which the chief effect is derived from the liquid applied. Examples: cold water sponging, alcohol rub, soap wash.

7. Rubs and Frictions. These are procedures in which the chief effect is derived from friction with the bare hands. Examples: centripetal friction, oil rub.

8. Baths. Under this heading are included various local and general procedures in which the body is immersed in water, light, heated air, or vapor. Examples: tub bath, foot bath, electric light and Russian baths.

9. Shampoos. The term "shampoo" applies to local or general cleansing measures by means of soap and water. (It is sometimes applied to massage.) Examples: Swedish shampoo, Turkish shampoo.

10. Packs. A pack is a procedure in which a considerable portion of the body is enveloped in wet sheets or blankets for therapeutic purposes. Examples: hot blanket pack, hot hip-and-leg pack, wet sheet pack.

11. Sprays and Douches. A spray or douche consists in the projection of one or more streams of water against the body. Examples: shower bath, needle spray, pail pour, hot and cold douche.

12. Enemata. An enema is an injection of fluid into the lower bowel. Examples: warm enema, rectal irrigation, coloclyster, oil enema, starch enema.

13. Vaginal Douches. The vaginal douche consists in the flushing or irrigating of the vaginal cavity with a fluid. Examples: hot vaginal irrigation, disinfectant douches, styptic douche.

REMEDIAL PROPERTIES OF WATER

The terms listed below are commonly used to designate the various physiologic or therapeutic effects of water. The definitions given should be studied thoroughly and memorized:

1. Tonic. A tonic effect is one in which vital activities are increased so as to restore the body to a normal tone or condition. The nutrition, circulation, and other body functions are promoted.

2. Pure Stimulant. A stimulant will arouse the body to unusual activities. It may be compared to a whip, and is used chiefly in emergencies. Like a tonic, it increases vital activities, but to a much greater degree. Between a pure stimulant and a tonic there are various gradations which might be designated as mild stimulant, extreme tonic, etc.

3. Sedative. A sedative or calmative agent is one which lessens vital activity and is conducive to relaxation and rest.

4. Antispasmodic. Relaxing of spasm or relieving of convulsions.

5. Depressant. A depressant effect is one in which heightened or normal body activities are decreased to a marked degree. Such an effect is desirable only where a function is greatly overactive.

6. Anodyne. An anodyne effect refers to the relief of pain.

7. **Spoliative.** A spoliative treatment is one which increases the oxidation and breaking down (katabolism) of tissues, tending to reduce weight.

8. **Diaphoretic.** An agent that produces sweating is said to have a diaphoretic or sudorific effect.

9. **Diuretic.** Increasing the excretion of urine.

10. **Eliminative.** An eliminative effect con sists in promoting and hastening excretion from the kidneys (diuresis), skin (diaphoresis), and lungs.

11. **Depletion.** Depletion is the lessening of the amount of blood in a given part. Practically it is the reduction of congestion.

12. **Derivative.** Derivation is the drawing of blood or lymph from one part of the body by increasing the amount in another part. The term "depletion" is also applied to this process, but refers particularly to the result produced.

13. **Fluxion.** Fluxion consists in greatly increasing the rapidity of the blood current in a particular part. It is the production of active or arterial hyperæmia.

14. **Antipyretic.** Lowering the body temperature in fever.

15. **Refrigerant.** Relieving of thirst and restoring the alkalinity of the blood by such means as free water-drinking and the use of fruit juices.

16. **Revulsive.** A term used to designate a treatment consisting of a single prolonged application of heat followed by a single very brief application of cold. This meaning is not strictly adhered to, as the term is also used where three applications of such proportionate duration are made.

17. **Alternate.** The expression "alternate hot and cold" is used in this text to describe treatments in which the duration of the cold application is from one fourth to one half that of the heat (in a few cases, equal to it), and in which three or more changes from heat to cold are made.

Common Names of Temperatures

"Heat" and "cold" are comparative, not absolute terms, and must needs be defined. This cannot be done with accuracy, since people differ in their toleration of heat and cold. The sensation produced varies according to the condition of the skin, its previous temperature, vigor of circulation, season of year, etc. We have therefore defined the usual limits in terms of degrees as follows:

Very hot - - - - -	104°	F. and above
Hot - - - - - -	100° to	104° F.
Warm (neutral 94° to 97°) -	92° to	100° F.
Tepid - - - - - -	80° to	92° F.
Cool - - - - - -	70° to	80° F.
Cold - - - - - -	55° to	70° F.
Very cold - - - - -	32° to	55° F.

LOCAL APPLICATIONS OF HEAT

Fomentations—Fo. A fomentation is a local application of moist heat by means of cloths wrung from hot water.

1. Articles Necessary. In well equipped treatment rooms, the fomentation tank should be so arranged that the water from which the fomentations are to be wrung, can be heated by a coil of live steam. When properly arranged, the escape of steam from this coil into the water will be noiseless, and cause the water to boil more vigorously than over a fire. A wringer with extra long rollers should be clamped to the side or end of the tank, and a table placed immediately beyond the wringer, on which the fomentations may be wrapped. If treatment is given at the patient's residence, a boiler or pail of hot water may be used. In an institution, it is rarely necessary to carry a pail of hot water to the patient's room, as the fomentations will be hotter if prepared in the treatment rooms and packed in a pail in the manner described hereafter. The nurse should also be provided with a set of six fomentation cloths, two Turkish towels for drying the patient, one large cotton sheet for covering the patient, a bowl of cold water or ice water, and one or two hand towels. An oilcloth and extra sheets and towels will be necessary to protect the bedding. If the treatment is to be given in a patient's room, provide a grass mat on which the pail of fomentations or hot water may be placed. If the pail is placed on a carpet, a newspaper may be all that is required. When the pail is set on a chair with a newspaper under it, the heat causes the paper to stick to the varnish.

2. The Patient. All clothing should be removed. If the clothing is not removed, then bare a larger area than the part to be treated, and thoroughly protect the clothing by thick Turkish towels. See that the feet are warm, and kept so during the treatment. If they are cold, a hot foot bath should be given, or hot-water bottles applied. The hot foot bath is much more effective than any other means of warming the feet.

In giving fomentations to a bed patient, great care should be exercised to avoid steaming the bedding, as a patient may easily take cold because of bed linen left damp after treatment. Protect the bedding underneath the patient by oilcloth, sheets, and towels, as necessary. After applying a fomentation, cover it with another dry fomentation cloth or a newspaper, in order to protect the bedding over the patient.

3. The Fomentation. Prepare a set of four or six fomentation cloths, thirty to thirty-six inches square. Four of these may be cut from a single blanket. The material should be half wool. Three cloths are necessary for one fomentation where they are to be very hot—one for the dry clothing, and two to be wrung from boiling water for the inside wet part. Where less heat is required, one inside cloth may be sufficient. Two such fomentations are necessary, if the best results are to be obtained. Spread out on the table the cloth for the dry covering. Fold together in three thicknesses so as to make a long, narrow piece, the cloth or cloths to be used inside. Holding the strip by one end, immerse in the boiling water. When thoroughly saturated with the boiling water, pass it quickly through the wringer, and after further folding or readjusting to the proper shape and size for the part to be treated, fold it quickly inside the dry fomentation cloth. It is now ready for use. By again doubling together the surface of the fomentation to be applied to the patient, it can be carried with less loss of heat. The fomentation should be large enough to cover a much larger area than the part affected.

Where it is necessary to wring the fomentation by hand, partially twist the long folded piece while it is held doubled together with one hand holding each end. Both ends are now grasped in one hand, and the fomentation dipped into the boiling water. When it is ready to wring, twist tightly, handling the fomentation cloth by the dry ends. Next, pull the ends apart. The water is thus squeezed out. The twisting and pulling may be repeated as necessary for thorough wringing of the cloth. By re-leasing one end while holding up the cloth by the other, it may be quickly untwisted and at once wrapped in the dry covering.

Where it is necessary to give the treatment in the patient's room, a set of three fomentations may be packed in a papier-mâché pail in such a way as to preserve their heat for a half hour or even longer. First, line the pail with large, dry fomentation cloths. Prepare each fomentation as usual, and pack in tightly, or, better still, wring by hand the inside cloths, leaving them twisted as tightly as possible, and pack closely in the lined pail. A hot-water bottle may be placed in the bottom of the pail if thought necessary, and another over the wet cloths. The necessary number of dry fomentation cloths may be packed into the top of the pail, and the fomentations made up in the room as needed.

4. Procedure. The fomentation should lie closely in contact with the skin, and be renewed in three or four minutes, or in case of pain, as soon as it becomes comfortable. If unbearably hot, rub the part with the hand under the fomentation, or re-move the moisture by firm rubbing once or twice with a Turkish towel wrapped about the hand. The fomentations may be applied over a towel in order to temper the heat. Always be careful to protect from chilling, the area being treated by keeping it covered with the fomentation cloth or a towel.

To renew the fomentation, prepare another simi-lar one, and apply immediately after removing the moisture occasioned by the first. Never apply an-other fomentation until this is done, as the water on the skin makes it more difficult to endure the heat of the newly prepared fomentation. The sec-

ond fomentation should be ready to apply before
the first is removed. The removal of the inside
cloth from the outer for purposes of renewal does
not give the best results, although careful attention to details may still make the treatment very
effective.

Unless otherwise indicated or ordered, three suc-
cessive applications are made. In all cases, however, they should be continued until the desired
effect is obtained. After the last one, the part
should be immediately cooled by a wet hand rub,
cold compress, or rub with a cold wet towel. Dry
thoroughly, and cover at once to prevent chilling.
In some cases of pain, the part should be dried
without the cold applications. All changes should
be made quickly, and the part treated should never
be left uncovered.

5. Precautions. In cases of unconsciousness,
paralyzed sensation, diabetes, dropsy, under anæsthesia or after operations, great care must be taken
to avoid burning. The degree of each application
should be tested by the back of the hand or by the
face before being applied to the patient. In fomentations to the face or other sensitive part, gauze
should be placed next to the skin.

In case of general perspiration, a general cold
friction, a wet hand rub, a wet towel rub, or an
alcohol rub should be given.

Sensitive surfaces, especially bony prominences,
such as the ilia, the costal arches, the clavicle, or
the scapula, may need to be protected by extra
coverings of flannel or Turkish towel.

When the patient is liable to cerebral congestion,
and always in case of fever, apply cold compresses
to the head, and also to the neck if needed. The
same should be done where two or more applica-

tions of heat are made at the same time, or general perspiration is induced. In case of heart disease, usually in fever, and with rapid pulse from any cause, an ice bag should be placed over the heart.

In order to relieve pain, the fomentation must be very hot, as hot as can be borne, and renewed as soon as it becomes comfortable. In some cases of pain, the cold application at the close should be omitted, the part being dried and immediately covered with flannel or other dry covering.

For sanitary reasons, it is desirable that each patient furnish his own fomentation cloths. However, persons with communicable diseases should not be admitted to a general treatment room.

6. Effects. The fomentation is used to relieve pain, produce derivation, as a preparation for cold treatment, and for stimulating or sedative effects, according to the temperature and the mode of application. Its first effect is that of a vital stimulant. Unless it is followed by a cold application, the reaction is atonic. A brief application is stimulating; prolonged applications are sedative or depressing. For sedative effects, the heat should be moderate, and the application more prolonged before renewal. These points should be observed in applying fomentations to the spine for insomnia.

Hot Gauze Compress—H. Comp. This is used to apply moist heat to such sensitive parts as the eye, a wound, or an infected part where the cloth must be disinfected or discarded after being used.

Several thicknesses of gauze, cheesecloth, or ordinary cotton cloth of appropriate size and shape, are wrung from boiling water and applied in the same way as a fomentation. Because the compress is usually small and unprotected, it cools quickly; and for this reason, it must be frequently renewed. Nor does cotton hold heat as long as wool. From ten to fifteen minutes will usually suffice to obtain the desired result. The treatment should be concluded in a manner similar to the fomentation.

Stupes. A stupe consists in the application of a medicament by means of a fomentation. When gauze compresses are used, the disinfectant or medicament may be put into the hot water from which the compress is wrung. In case of a large fomentation with flannel cloths, the medicament may be applied by compresses placed under the fomentation. Turpentine, mustard, menthol, etc., may be used in this way. However, the desired hyperæmia and depletion can usually be obtained in a more cleanly manner by a plain fomentation, and without the danger of a blister. A stupe does not require as close attention or as frequent renewal as the fomentation. Doubtless this is the reason why it is so much used in hospitals.

In preparing the gauze or muslin for the mustard fomentation, use one teaspoonful of mustard to a cup of hot water. Spread out this mustard compress on the surface to be treated, and cover with an ordinary fomentation.

Revulsive Compress—Rev. Comp. This is given in the same manner as the fomentation, with the addition of a cold compress after each application of heat. A hand towel is wrung from cold water or ice water, according to the ability of the patient to react. This towel is spread out over the surface immediately on the removal of the fomentation, and is allowed to remain about thirty seconds. The skin is then dried, and the next fomentation is applied. Three changes of hot and three of cold are usually employed. The revulsive compress is a mild stimulant and tonic measure. It also produces mild fluxion in the part treated.

Alternate Hot and Cold to Spine—H. & C. Sp. Fomentations are given in the same manner as for the revulsive compress. After each, a smooth piece of ice is quickly rubbed back and forth over the part, making from three to five or more to-and-fro movements. The part is then dried, and another fomentation is applied. In the making of these hot and cold applications, the next fomentation should be ready before the ice is applied.

Alternate hot and cold applications may be made to other parts in the same manner.

Alternate hot and cold to the spine is a vigorous stimulant and tonic measure, and is useful in a great variety of conditions.

Alternate Hot and Cold to Head—H. & C. Hd. *1. Articles Necessary.* Two compresses of three to five thicknesses of gauze or cheesecloth about twelve inches square.

Two ice bags filled with finely chopped ice and covered with cheesecloth.

A spine bag partly filled with hot water and covered with a fomentation cloth or a towel.

A bowl of ice water and a pail of boiling water.

2. Procedure. Place the spine bag crosswise of the cervical spine, bringing it well up under back of head and neck.

Lightly wring cheesecloth from ice water and apply to face, covering top of head and ears. Press down firmly over forehead and temporal arteries. Renew every minute.

After three minutes, replace the spine bag by two cloth-covered ice bags, and the cold compress to the face by another wrung quite dry from hot water. The latter should be renewed every minute. In another three minutes, repeat the first applications of spine bag to the back of the neck and cold compress to the face. Continue these alternations for three complete sets of hot and cold. Cool all the parts by wiping off with a cold compress, and dry thoroughly, especially the hair.

3. Effect. These alternating hot and cold applications stimulate the cerebral circulation, and the treatment is therefore indicated in headache due to anæmia of the brain, also in passive congestion and in a cold in the head. Any alternating hot and cold application produces *fluxion.*

Simultaneous Hot and Cold to Head— Simul. H. & C. Hd. Place an ice bag to the base of the brain, and another ice bag, or better, an ice cap, to the vertex, after moistening the hair so that the cold will penetrate. Also place ice bags or ice compresses over the carotids. Now apply a fomentation to the face, covering the ears and the forehead. Gauze or cheesecloth should be used under the fomentation applied to the face. The fomentation should not cover the nose, as it is uncomfortable when so applied, and the patient would better be permitted to breathe cooler air.

This treatment is very effective in reducing cerebral congestion and relieving congestive headache. It is well to conclude the treatment by an alternate hot and cold percussion douche to the feet, cold cervical and cephalic compresses being kept on during the douche.

Simultaneous applications of heat and cold so given that the cold application is placed over a reflex area of, or the large artery supplying, the deep part produce *depletion.*

Hot-Water Bottles. These should be partly filled with hot water (never boiling water) and

2—Hydrotherapy

wrapped in cloth, preferably flannel or a Turkish towel. Great care should be taken in applying them to patients with paralysis and during and after operations, that burns do not result. The safety of the hot-water bottle may be tested by holding it against the cheek. When not in use, the bottle should be hung bottom end up, with the stopper out. It should never be left doubled sharply upon itself, as it is likely to crack at the fold.

Fomentations may be reënforced or prolonged by the use of hot-water bottles, or the bag may be wrapped in a moist cloth covered over by a dry one, to give the effects of a mild fomentation.

Winternitz Coil. This consists of a matted coil of rubber tubing about ten or eleven inches in diameter, through which a stream of hot water is caused to flow. A dry blanket is placed on the treatment table, and over this is placed a doubled sheet, wrung from cold water or ice water, so that it may be wrapped about the trunk. The patient lies down on the wet sheet, and one end is wrapped tightly about the chest and the abdomen. The coil is now placed on the abdomen over the wet sheet, and the other end of the sheet is wrapped around the trunk over the coil. The dry blanket is folded over and about the patient. A small stream of hot water at 135° flows slowly through the coil from the center outward. The treatment is continued from thirty to forty minutes, or even three hours in cases of very slow and defective digestion. It is concluded by a cold mitten friction. A hot-water bottle may be used in place of the coil. (See Hot and Heating Trunk Pack.)

The coil may be used for cold water in the same manner as the Leïter coil. In fact, the cold coil is much more frequently used, and for a greater number of purposes, than the hot coil.

Radiant Heat—Rad. Heat. The radiant heat is a local application of heat by means of electric lights arranged in a reflecting metal case. From one to twelve or more such lights may be arranged in a single case, and the case so constructed as to fit to any part of the body. An instrument with one light is perhaps the most useful. An oblong case containing three lights is a convenient means of applying heat to the spine. A case in the shape of a half cylinder, and containing six or more lights, may be made for the feet and the legs.

In the application of radiant heat, the body should be protected from the edge of the case by towels or fomentation cloths. The amount of heat may be regulated by the number of lights or the distance from the skin. Leave in place for ten to twenty minutes, or until the desired results are obtained. Cover the part well after drying perspiration, or use a cold wet towel. The local electric light is a convenient means of applying heat to the feet, the knees, and other joints. It may also be used over bandages, to avoid removing them.

LOCAL APPLICATIONS OF COLD

Cold Compress—C. Comp. A cold compress is a local application of cold by means of a cloth wrung from cold water. Hand towels or ordinary cotton cloths may be used. These should be folded to the desired size, and wrung from cold water or ice water. The wringing should be just sufficient to prevent dripping. They will be colder if taken immediately from a block of ice. As a continuous cold application, the compress must be very frequently renewed, always before it is warmed to any great extent. The thicker the compress, the less frequently will it require renewal. A set of two compresses should be used, and renewed at intervals of from one to five minutes, depending on the thickness of the compress and the result to be obtained. Cold compresses may be applied to the head, the neck, over the heart or the lungs, to the abdomen, the spine, etc. When applied to the head, they should be pressed down firmly on the surface treated, especially over the forehead and the temporal arteries. The pillow should be protected by rubber cloth covered by a towel. When compresses are applied to the abdomen in typhoid fever, the bedding and the patient's garments should be protected by Turkish towels. Unless the compress is very thick, and always when left longer than three to five minutes, the nature of the application changes, and it becomes a *heating compress.*

When applied over a large artery, it decreases the amount of blood in the part beyond the application. Such an application is called a *proximal compress.* Examples of this are found in such applications as a cold compress to the neck, over the femoral artery, at the bend of the elbow, etc. Ice bags are also used for the same purpose.

Ice Pack—Ice Pk. An ice pack is used where a large, continuous, and very cold application is desired. Spread cracked ice over a thick Turkish towel, folding one end and the edges over this so as to retain the ice. Apply next to the skin or over a single layer of flannel. This may be used over the heart, also over a consolidated lung area in pneumonia. In the latter case, it should never be applied until after the hot packs used in this disease have warmed the body sufficiently to prevent chilling. It should occasionally be interrupted by the application of a fomentation. This helps to preserve the desired reflex effect.

Snow may be used in place of the pounded ice. In applying an ice pack to a joint, first wrap the part in flannel, so as to prevent actual freezing, then pack the snow or pounded ice closely against the flannel, forming a layer about one inch thick, retaining it in place by a larger flannel cloth wrapped about all and pinned together.

Ice packs should be interrupted often enough to prevent freezing, and either the part rubbed with snow or a fomentation applied to renew the local reaction.

Ice Cravat. The ice cravat or collar is made in the same way as the ice pack, the towel being filled with ice and folded so as to be about three inches wide and encircle the neck. If the towel is wrung from ice water, it must be more frequently renewed than when cracked ice is used. An ice cravat may also be made by using two narrow spinal ice bags. These should be filled with pounded ice and wrapped in a linen or cotton cloth.

The effect is that of a proximal application. The carotid arteries and their distal branches are contracted, also the vertebral arteries. Thus the blood supply to the brain and the head generally is very much lessened. The ice collar is frequently used in fever, in congestive headache, in acute epidemic meningitis, etc. It should also be used in sunstroke, and whenever prolonged sweating treatments are given, as in eclampsia and uræmia.

Ice Bag and Ice Cap—Ice Bg. Ice bags are made in various shapes and sizes. The best ice bags are made of pure gum rubber, and are usually elliptical in shape. They may be obtained in almost any size desired. The spinal ice bag is about three inches wide by seven to nine or ten long. Ice caps are usually round or elliptical and provided with a screw cap. Some are also made with loops for holding them in place. Cloth-covered ice bags offer no advantage. They usually leak after being used a few times, and are unsanitary. The ice bag or cap should be filled with finely cracked or pounded ice, never with large chunks. In the case of the ice bag, the neck should be doubled down, then folded several times across this, and tied with tape about one fourth inch wide. Thread or fine twine should not be used, as it cuts the rubber. When applying the bag, wrap it in a towel or one thickness of flannel. The skin should not be severely chilled. The bag should be removed often enough to prevent this, the part rubbed briskly with the hand until warmed, or a fomentation applied for a short time.

Cold Water Coil—C. Coil. The rubber coil (Winternitz coil) is the most convenient means of making a local application of cold. Matted coils, ten or eleven inches in diameter, may be purchased, or a coil may be made of ordinary rubber tubing and held together by adhesive tapes. The inflow should enter at the center of the coil. The rate of flow may be very conveniently controlled by a knot in the outflow tube just above where it dips into the receiving pail. This knot may be loose or tight, as desired for rapid or slow flowing of the cold water through the coil. The reservoir should be about two feet above the level of the coil, and may be a large can with an outlet at the bottom, or an ordinary pail may be used, and the outflow secured by siphonage.

The coil should always be applied over a cold compress, and covered with a dry flannel cloth or a dry fomentation cloth. When applied to the head, the coil may be molded into the shape of a cap, and held in place by light bandages or folded towels. Always wet the hair before placing the coil. The Leiter coil is not used as much as the rubber coil. It is a small, flat coil of flexible metal tubing, through which a stream of cold water or ice water passes. It may be molded to fit any part, and is often used over the mastoid. The principle is the same as that of the Winternitz coil.

HEATING COMPRESSES

A heating compress is a cold compress so covered that warming up soon occurs. The effect is therefore that of a mild application of moist heat.

A heating pack or compress consists of an application of heat to the body by means of three or four thicknesses of gauze or one of linen or cotton cloth wrung from cold water and so perfectly covered with dry flannel or mackintosh and flannel as to prevent the circulation of air and cause an accumulation of body heat. In case warming does not occur promptly, it should be aided by hot-water bottles or the radiant heat. It is usually left in place for several hours between other treatments, or overnight. If left on overnight, it should be dry by morning unless an impervious covering, such as mackintosh or oiled silk, is used. On removal of the compress, the part should be rubbed with cold water.

According to the extent and location of the surface involved, the nature and thickness of the coverings, the temperature and the amount of water left in the wet cloth, and the duration of the application, it may have the following effects: tonic, sedative, derivative, sweating.

If the pack dries out before being removed, it

will have a mild derivative and a mild sedative or tonic effect, according to the part to which it is applied and the condition in which it is used. If the coverings prevent drying, the result will be that of a stronger derivative because of the local sweating. It also causes relaxation of the muscles and vasodilatation of the vessels in immediate or reflex relation with the surface treated.

Moist Chest Pack—Ch. Pk. Any kind of jacket that combines the above requisites for a heating compress with ease and neatness of application and accuracy of fit, will answer the purpose of a chest pack.

The roller, square, and fitted chest packs are examples of these.

1. ROLLER CHEST PACK. The inside piece consists of two to five thicknesses of gauze eight to ten inches wide and about six or eight feet in length. One thickness of thin linen may be used. The outside piece of flannel is a little wider than the gauze and somewhat longer. The gauze or linen is loosely rolled in bandage form, and wrung nearly dry from cold water. While standing in front of the patient, apply the end under one arm, more handily the right, then carry diagonally across the front of the chest and over the left shoulder, then obliquely across the back, under the right arm, and directly across the front of the chest, under the left arm, across the back, and over the right shoulder, and fasten under the transverse front piece. The bandage must be snugly applied at all places, but not so tight as to restrict the movements of the chest. The flannel is now applied in the same order, care being taken that the wet piece is well covered, and then securely fastened with safety pins. The pack should be comfortable and feel warm in a very short time.

2. SQUARE CHEST PACK. Both parts of the pack are of an oblong form, wide enough to reach from the top of the shoulder to the lower ribs, and long enough to give a double thickness in front. The ends of the bandage are slit into two strips one third and two thirds, respectively, of the total width, and each one third of the length. The outer flannel part should be about two inches wider, and of the same length, and slit in the same fashion. The flannel part should be spread out on the treatment table, and the linen over it after being wrung from cold water. The patient now lies back on this. The narrow strips are brought over the shoulder and across the chest. The top of the wider strips should fit under the axilla and be brought across the chest. The flannel should now be applied in the same manner, and at all loose places, be drawn tight or folded in, and the whole fastened with safety pins.

3. FITTED CHEST PACK. From flannel, cut a front and a back piece in much the same shape as for a vest, making the necessary curved cuts about the arms and the neck. The front piece should be the larger, so as to come back under the arms and lap over the back piece; also on each side of the neck, a strip four inches wide should be made long enough to overlap the back piece.

An inside piece of the same shape should be cut from gauze or thin linen. This inside piece should be about one and one half inches narrower at all edges, so that when covered by the flannel, it will not be exposed at any place, but be covered at least one inch beyond its edge.

After applying, see that it fits snugly and is well pinned with safety pins, so as to prevent the entrance of air at any place along the edges.

Various other forms may be improvised to meet

the needs of the home not provided with the more perfect requisites. To retain the moisture and so give greater sweating effects, the cloth may be covered with mackintosh, gossamer cloth, or oiled silk, of the same size and shape. When so covered, it is called a *protected chest pack*.

4. PARTIAL CHEST PACK. It is often desirable to apply the moist cloth to only a portion of the chest. The gauze or linen may be cut to any desired shape and size, and applied to the proper area under the square or roller flannel pack. The chest being covered principally by dry flannel, this form approaches in effect the dry pack.

Dry Chest Pack—Dry Ch. Pk. With the dry chest pack, only the flannel is used, of either the roller, the square, or the fitted style. It should usually be applied over a thin undergarment. The dry chest pack is desirable in thin persons, the aged, and those having insufficient body heat to warm up the wet pack. In the case of a thin person, it is often difficult, not to say impossible, to **pin the wet pack so tightly as to prevent the air** from circulating under the edges of the pack, and yet loose enough to be comfortable and not restrict the breathing. In many cases, a chamois vest may be worn over a thin undergarment, to produce the effects of a dry pack. The commonly used pneumonia jacket made of absorbent cotton wrapped in gauze or of similar construction is one form of the dry pack.

Chest packs are of much benefit in pleurisy, pneumonia, colds, influenza of the respiratory type, during convalescence from pneumonia, in asthma, in whooping cough, croup, etc. Under the pack, the skin should be warm and gently perspiring. The choice of a dry or a moist pack will depend upon the vitality of the patient and the result to be obtained.

Moist Abdominal Bandage—M. A. B. 'The moist abdominal girdle is one of the most useful of the heating compresses. The inside part of the girdle consists of one thickness of linen or three or four of gauze, eight or nine inches wide and a little more than one and one half times the circumference of the body. The outer flannel girdle should be about twelve inches wide and of the same length. The dry flannel is placed across the table, and the gauze, wrung nearly dry from cold water, placed over it. The patient now lies back on the bandage so that the lower edge will be below the iliac crests. Each end of the wet linen or gauze is pulled tightly across the abdomen and tucked under the opposite side. Both ends of the flannel are folded tightly over these and securely fastened with safety pins. Darts may be taken on each side by means of safety pins, in the same manner as in pinning a bandage after an abdominal operation. The flannel piece should project one and one half or two inches beyond the wet gauze or linen. Where the patient cannot easily warm up the bandage, it may be moistened only over the abdomen.

The moisture may be retained by a bandage of oiled silk or mackintosh of the same width as the linen, and applied between it and the flannel. This is termed a protected girdle.

The sweating underneath will be more profuse than without the impervious covering. Since the moisture is retained, the girdle will not be dry by morning. The protected girdle is indicated in hyperacidity, and where it is desirable to produce considerable relaxation.

The ordinary moist abdominal bandage is useful

in nearly all forms of atonic indigestion, in neurasthenia, anæmia of the liver, insomnia, catarrhal jaundice, constipation, etc.   In these conditions, it is usually worn only at night.

Heating Throat Compress. Four to six thicknesses of cheesecloth, or two or three of ordinary cotton cloth, about three inches wide, and long enough to encircle the neck twice, are used inside. The outside consists of two thicknesses of flannel not less than four inches wide. This compress being small, considerable water may be left in it, and still it be found dry by morning. The neck should be rubbed with cold water immediately after the removal of the compress in the morning. The ''cold cloth around the neck'' is a very common household remedy for sore throat, hoarseness, tonsillitis, etc. It is indeed a very efficient measure. Its usefulness can hardly be overestimated. The heating throat compress is indicated in pharyngitis, acute laryngitis, tonsillitis, quinsy, and in inflammation of the Eustachian tube. It is also useful in clergyman's sore throat. In tonsillitis, quinsy, and inflammation of the Eustachian tube, the compress should extend upward about the lower part of the ear, and may be held in place by a bandage over the top of the head.

Heating Joint Compress. Heating compresses may be applied to the foot, the ankle, the knee, the hand, the wrist, etc. Rarely more than two thicknesses of gauze are used. It is often necessary to use cotton for a covering to obtain close application to the skin surface. This may be held in place by a three-inch roller bandage or a broad flannel cloth. A dry pack may be made of cotton or soft flannel alone. In certain cases, the joints may be rubbed with a medicated solution before being covered, or the gauze dipped in it. Alkaline or anodyne solutions are very frequently used in this way in cases of rheumatism. In rheumatic fever, the joints may be rubbed with synthetic oil of wintergreen before the heating compress is applied. It helps to relieve the pain; and by its action as a counterirritant, the heating and circulatory effects are enhanced.

Medicated Compresses. Not only may the parts be rubbed with medicaments, such as turpentine, camphorated oil, oil of wintergreen, etc., before the heating compress or pack is applied, but the gauze may be wrung from various solutions, such as an alcoholic solution of menthol, mustard water, watery solution of bicarbonate of soda, saltpeter, etc. When counterirritant drugs are used, the effect of the heating compress is intensified. It is usually not desirable to produce a blister. For this reason, the use of coal oil and turpentine should be discouraged. Not only may they produce blisters, but being inflammable, they are also dangerous.

POULTICES

Poultices are very popular substitutes for the heating compress, and have a similar effect. They consist of a mixture of various substances having the consistency of mush, and must be applied hot to produce the desired result. Flaxseed, onions, etc., are commonly used. The preparation may be applied directly to the skin, or spread on a cloth and bound tightly to the part. Poultices are often disagreeable, not to say uncleanly.

Probably the most useful poultice is that consisting of *white clay and glycerin*, sold under various names. It is applied hot about one quarter to one half inch thick, and covered with cotton and a bandage. The results are partly due to the heat and partly to the water-absorbing (hygroscopic) properties of glycerin.

The *charcoal* poultice is especially valuable in foul, sloughing ulcers or wounds. It may be prepared of charcoal alone, or by adding equal parts of flaxseed meal and powdered charcoal to boiling water until the resulting mixture is the consistency of mush. This is evenly spread on a cloth and applied to the part, or directly on the part, and covered with a muslin cloth, and some impervious cloth, as oiled silk.

TONIC FRICTIONS

A tonic friction is an application of cold water so combined with friction as to produce decided thermic and circulatory reaction. The effects are briefly described as stimulant and tonic. These terms have been defined elsewhere.

Given in the order of their severity, the tonic frictions are as follows: wet hand rub, cold mitten friction, cold towel rub, wet sheet rub, and dripping sheet rub. To these may be added the ice rub and the salt glow. While the latter is not particularly an application of cold, the friction gives tonic results similar to the others, and the procedure is not far different. The ice rub may be used for stimulant or tonic purposes, but it is more frequently used as an antipyretic.

Cold Mitten Friction—C. M. F. or Cmf.
1. Articles Required. A bowl or pail of cold water at 50° or 60° F. or ice water, a sheet, three Turkish towels, two friction mitts made of such coarse material as woolen moreen, and compresses for the head and the neck.

2. Procedure. The patient should be warmly covered and the feet warm; if not, give a hot foot bath. Bare one part of the body at a time. Do not expose any part longer than necessary; dry quickly and thoroughly, and cover at once with warm, dry covering. Before beginning the regular part of the treatment, bathe the patient's face and neck with cold water, or apply cold compresses to the head and the neck. This is especially necessary in treating patients with valvular heart disease. In this condition, an ice bag should be placed over the heart before the treatment is begun. In other conditions, it is not usually necessary.

Beginning with the right arm, place one towel under the arm, and another around the shoulder, to protect the table and the patient. With the mitts on the hands, dip them into cold water, and shake or squeeze out the excess of water. While the patient holds the arm at an angle of forty-five degrees, rub the arm and the hand with rapid to-and-fro friction movements until it is in a glow. Quickly remove the mitts, dropping them into the bowl, and cover the entire arm with one of the Turkish towels, steadying the arm by grasping the patient's hand under the operator's arm. Dry by friction outside the towel, and then rub with the towel until the arm is thoroughly dry and well reddened. Treat the left arm in the same manner.

• Now covering the rest of the body, bare the chest and the abdomen. Tuck a Turkish towel snugly under each side along the trunk and over the arms. Rub the chest with the mitten dipped in cold water, in a manner similar to the arms. Then cover the entire chest with one of the towels, and have the patient catch the two upper corners as they lie next to the shoulders. Rub briskly with downward strokes over the towel. Then wrapping the towel neatly about the right hand, again rub the entire surface, around the shoulders, and down the sides, so as to dry all parts that have been wet.

Cover the chest, and expose the right leg and thigh. Flex the leg, and place a Turkish towel under. Place another towel around the upper thigh at the groin. Begin the friction with the leg and the foot. Dip the mitts again for the thigh. Treat in like manner the left leg and thigh.

Have the patient turn over and lie on a pillow placed under the chest. Treat the back in the same manner as the front of the trunk. To dry, cover the entire back with a Turkish towel, and have the patient hold the upper end the same as for the chest; rub with downward strokes over the towel, then wrap the towel about the hand, and rub the surface again until thoroughly dry. Some prefer to begin the treatment with the chest in cases of heart disease.

To vary the severity and the tonic effects, the temperature of the water may be changed, more may be left in the mitts, or the mitts may be dipped two or three times in treating each part, or the friction may be given more vigorously.

Wet Hand Rub—W. H. R. or Whr. The same order and general procedure is followed as for the cold mitten friction. Bare one part at a time, rub with the hand dipped in cold water, following with percussion, then dry, finishing with brisk rubbing with the dry towel and the hands. Dipping from two to four or more times increases the tonic effect.

Cold Towel Rub—C. T. R. or Ctr. In giving the cold towel rub, a plain hand towel is used instead of the mitts employed for the cold mitten friction. The same order is followed as in the two previous treatments, beginning with the arms, then the chest and the abdomen, the legs, and last, the back.

The arm is held vertically, with the palm toward the feet. The towel is dipped in cold water and wrung lightly, quickly unfolded, and wrapped lengthwise around the arm, the upper corners being turned into the palm to be grasped by the hand of the patient. The part is then rubbed with to-and-fro movements outside the towel. Percussion may also be given, to insure greater reaction. The towel is now removed, and the arm dried as after the cold mitten friction.

When the chest and the abdomen are treated, the wet towel is spread out over the entire surface, and the patient grasps the upper corners next the shoulders, and holds tightly while the nurse rubs with downward strokes outside the towel. The other parts are treated in a similar manner.

It should be remembered that the cold towel rub takes more heat from the body than the cold mitten friction, and it therefore requires greater reactive ability on the part of the patient. Because it does abstract considerable heat from the body, it is often used in fever as an antipyretic measure. By dipping the towel twice or more for a single part, its antipyretic effects are increased.

Wet Sheet Rub—W. Sh. R. *1. Requisites.* Two sheets, two towels, a tub containing hot water for the feet, a pail of water at 60° to 70° F. Other temperatures may be used when indicated.

2. Procedure. The patient should be warm to begin with. Apply a cold compress to the head. The patient now stands in the tub of hot water. A sheet is wrung from cold water so that it will not drip. Quickly wrap the sheet about the patient as follows:

3—Hydrotherapy

The patient holds up both arms. The upper left-hand corner of the sheet is placed under the patient's right arm; the patient then lowers the right arm, thus holding the corner of the sheet in place. Pass the sheet quickly across the front of the body and under the left arm, which is lowered. The sheet should then be carried across the back, behind and up over the right shoulder, then across the chest and around the neck over the left shoulder, the corner being tucked under the edge of the sheet behind. Now tuck the sheet between the patient's legs; it is thus brought into close contact with every portion of the skin. Rub vigorously and give percussion over the sheet, covering the whole surface as quickly as possible, until the sheet is thoroughly warmed. The patient is not to be rubbed *with* the sheet, but *over* the sheet. Two attendants are necessary to give the best results. Dry with a sheet and towels.

The wet sheet rub is a very vigorous tonic measure. It should not be used until the patient is able to react to the cold towel rub, the pail pour, and the cold percussion douche.

Dripping Sheet Rub—Drip. Sh. R. For the dripping sheet rub, prepare three pails of cold water at about 70°, 65°, 60° F. respectively. Proceed as with the wet sheet rub, using the water at 70° from which to wring the sheet. After the sheet and the patient are warmed by rubbing and percussion, without removing the sheet, pour over the shoulders the second pail of water, again rubbing vigorously until warm. Use the third pail in like manner. Dry as after the wet sheet rub.

Ice Rub. The order of parts treated and the procedure in an ice rub are substantially the same as in the wet hand rub and the cold mitten friction. In giving the ice rub, however, it is necessary to

protect the bed or the treatment table more thoroughly by covering with oilcloth and towels. Turkish
towels should be tucked closely about each part, so
as to absorb the water as it runs off the skin. The
cake of ice to be used may be held in the hand, or
better yet, wrapped in one or two thicknesses of
gauze.

The ice rub is not much used for general tonic
purposes, but more frequently as an antipyretic.
When it is used for this purpose, each part should
be rubbed for some time, and then dried without
friction or percussion with the hands. Its prolonged application to the spine is more decidedly
antipyretic than the same length of application
elsewhere. When this treatment is given in typhoid
fever, the abdomen should be avoided. Cold compresses should be applied to the head and the neck
and also to the heart, if necessary.

Salt Glow—Sgl. Prepare about two pounds of
coarse salt wet with cold water. The treatment
should be given in a ''wet room'' or in a bathtub.
The patient stands in a tub of hot water. While
standing at the side of the patient, begin with the
arm. Wet the entire skin surface of the shoulder,
the arm, and the hand with hot water from the foot
tub. This is done by dipping the water with the
hands. Next apply the wet salt, spreading it
evenly over the skin. Now with one hand on each
side of the arm, rub vigorously with to-and-fro
movements, until the skin is in a glow. Stepping
behind the patient to the opposite side, proceed in
the same manner with the other arm.

Retain the last position to treat the front and
back of the trunk. With one hand in front and
one behind, wet the skin surface with hot water
from the foot tub. Now spread the salt as before,
and rub the entire skin surface of the chest, the

abdomen, the shoulders, the back, and the buttocks.
Stepping behind the patient, with one hand under
each arm, continue rubbing with the salt, treating
the sides of the chest, the abdomen, and the hips.

Next proceed with the legs in like manner. For
each leg, have the patient put one foot on a low
stool, so as to bring the thigh about horizontal.
Wet with water as before, and rub the thigh, the
leg, and the foot with the wet salt.

Finish the treatment by thoroughly washing off
the salt. This may be done by a pail pour, a
shower, or a general spray. Dry the patient with
sheets, towels, and fanning with a dry sheet as
from any general wet treatment.

If for any reason the patient ought not to stand
so long, he may be seated on a low stool while the
salt glow is given. Proceed as follows:

The patient sits on a stool, with the feet in hot
water. Beginning with the feet and the legs, apply
the water and then the salt, rubbing briskly with
short strokes, the hands being on either side of the
part treated. Next treat each arm separately; then
the chest, the abdomen, and the back should be
rubbed with the wet salt, the attendant standing
at the side of the patient, with one hand rubbing
the chest, and the other rubbing the back. The
patient should stand while the buttocks and the
thighs are treated. Wash off the salt, and dry as
directed above.

The salt glow is a vigorous circulatory stimulant.
Since no great amount of cold water is applied
to the body, it does not require as great reactive
ability as the wet sheet rub or the cold douche.

SPONGING

Sponging consists in the application of a liquid
by means of a sponge, a cloth, or the bare hand,

in which the chief effect is derived from the liquid that is applied. The term ''ablution'' is also applied to sponging.

Plain Water Sponging—Spg. 1. HOT SPONGE —H. SPG. Hot sponging has a sedative effect because of the slightly atonic reaction that ensues. It is also used to reduce fever where chilliness exists. When it is prolonged to forty or fifty minutes, the temperature does not rise as rapidly after the treatment as after a cold sponge.

A large, soft sea sponge may be used, a soft cotton cloth, a wash cloth of Turkish toweling, or several thicknesses of cheesecloth. The water should be as hot as can be borne. Bare one part at a time, and treat in the following order: the arms, the chest, the abdomen, the legs, the thighs, and the back. The cloth or sponge should be dipped several times for each part. Dry thoroughly.

2. TEPID SPONGE—TEPID SPG. The tepid sponge has an effect similar to that of the neutral bath; that is, it is sedative. It may also be used to reduce fever, but is not as effective as either the hot or the cold sponge.

3. COOL OR COLD SPONGE—C. SPG. Cold sponging is much used in the treatment of fever where the skin is hot and there is no tendency to chilliness. Go over each part several times. The temperature of the water and the duration of the treatment should be governed by the effect to be produced.

Saline Sponge—Sal. Spg. About four ounces of common salt is dissolved in a basin or bowl of tepid water. The bare hand is dipped into the salt water, and each part is rubbed lightly.

The saline sponge has a mild tonic effect. Because of the salt, it stimulates the vasomotors to a greater extent than plain water does.

Alkaline Sponge—Alk. Spg. Use about two ounces of bicarbonate of soda to a small basin of hot or cool water, according to the case. Apply with the bare hand, a soft cloth, or a sponge. The alkaline sponge is useful in itching, smarting, and other abnormal sensations. It is usually applied only to the part affected.

Vinegar and Salt Rub. The vinegar and salt rub is very useful in checking the excessive perspiration or night sweats of phthisis.

Prepare a half pint of equal parts of vinegar and water, to which add one or two tablespoonfuls of salt. Apply with the bare hand, drying lightly afterward.

The application should be thorough to the parts that perspire the most; other parts may be treated less thoroughly.

Alcohol Rub—Alc. R. The alcohol rub is frequently used following a sweating treatment, instead of the cold friction or spray. Its purpose is, of course, the prevention of taking cold. Use one part of alcohol to one part of water (proof spirit, fifty per cent). Dip the hands in the alcohol, and rub each part, dipping the second time if needed. No drying with the towel is necessary.

Witch-Hazel Rub—Wzr. The witch-hazel rub has about the same effect as the alcohol rub. It is sedative and a mild astringent. The same procedure is used as for the alcohol rub.

Menthol Rub—Menth. R. The application of menthol to the skin gives a sensation of cold. The effect is similar to that of the alcohol rub or cold sponging. Use one ounce of menthol liniment (menthol cryst. 1 oz., alcohol 1 pint) to three or four ounces of water.

Soap Wash. The soap wash is used for cleansing the skin in the case of bed patients. Using a bowl of water at 102° F. with soap and wash cloth, go over each part separately. With another bowl of water at 75° to 85° F. and another cloth, remove the soapy water, and dry thoroughly with a Turkish towel. Go over each part with the soapy water, and follow by rinsing with plain cool water, then dry before treating the next part.

RUBS AND FRICTIONS

These terms are applied to procedures in which the chief effect is derived from friction with the bare hands.

Centripetal Friction—C. F. or cf. The centripetal friction consists principally in friction strokes from the periphery toward the center. It is designed to hasten the circulation, especially in the superficial veins.

GENERAL ORDER OF MOVEMENTS:

1. Light to-and-fro friction—once.
2. Apply lubricant—twice.
3. Centripetal friction—three times.
4. Percussion—twice.
5. Stroking (centrifugal)—three times.

Arms

1. Beginning at the finger tips, give light, quick to-and-fro friction to the shoulder, being sure to cover thoroughly the whole surface. Let the hands glide back as in stroking the arm.

2. Apply lubricant with long strokes from finger tips to shoulder, returning with four rotary sweeps. Give twice.

3. Friction.

Hand.

  a. Heavy centripetal stroking to back of hand, three times.

  b. Palm of hand same as back of hand, beginning at finger tips. Finish with double rotary movement in palm. Give three times.

Arm and forearm.

  a. Empty blood vessels by heavy, even stroking from wrist to elbow. The patient's elbow rests upon the table. With one hand on each side, and using the hands alternately, give three movements with each.

  b. Empty the blood vessels from elbow to shoulder, sweeping well over the shoulder. With the hands in the same position and alternating as for the forearm, give three movements with each.

  4. Percussion. With one hand on each side of the arm, which is held up by the patient, and with hands working together, give percussion from shoulder to fingers and return. Give twice. Place the patient's arm on the table at his side, and give percussion down and up to the external surface as far as the hand.

  5. Stroking—three times.

Legs

  1. Leg flexed and foot flexed. Placing one hand on the sole, the other on the dorsum of the foot, give light, quick to-and-fro friction transverse of the foot. Then placing the foot flat, continue with rapid strokes to the sides of the foot, the leg, and the front of the thigh. Glide the hands to the knee; quick strokes to the back of the thigh; glide to the toes.

2. Apply lubricant with long strokes to the back of the leg and the front of the thigh, coming down to the knee with three rotary sweeps, then long strokes to the back of the thigh, down with three rotary sweeps from knee to ankle. Give twice.

3. Friction.

Foot (leg extended).

   a. Dorsum with one hand—three times.

   b. Each side with one hand, the opposite hand supporting the foot; come well up back of the ankle—three times.

   c. The sole with the palm of the hand—three times.

   d. Rotary strokes to the heel—three times.

Leg and thigh (leg flexed).

   a. Calf—empty the blood vessels by heavy, even stroking, the hands following each other alternately—three times with each hand.

   b. Empty the blood vessels under the knee, the hands alternating—three times with each.

   c. With one hand on the knee to support the leg, give heavy stroking to the front of the leg, beginning at the toes—three times.

   d. Rotary to knee, the hands working together—three times.

   e. Empty the blood vessels of the thigh, beginning with the posterior surface, the hands working together—three times.

   f. Anterior thigh—three times.

4. Percussion. With one hand on each side, give percussion from hip to ankle, down and up. Give twice.

5. Stroking—three times.

Chest and Abdomen

1. Making the hands work together, stroke the neck downward three times, and give rotary movements as follows: three above the clavicle and to the shoulder; six from below the clavicle to the level of the elbow (that is, nine down each side), returning up over median part of abdomen and chest. Give once or twice.

2. Apply lubricant with long strokes up the center, four rotary sweeps down the sides, covering the whole surface thoroughly. Give twice.

3. Friction.

a. Empty the blood vessels of the neck and shoulders by stroking from back of the ears downward to the chest and the shoulders—three times.

b. Give strokes from the shoulders to the median line over the pectorals—three times.

c. Using the thumb and the thenar surface, give heavy strokes outward from the median line over the ribs and the abdomen—about six times, advancing toward the pubes.

d. Stroking from the umbilicus outward and downward toward the middle of Poupart's ligament—three times.

4. Percussion up and down the left side, the same on the right side. Give twice.

5. Stroking—three times.

Back

1. Light friction with the full hand down the spine, the hands alternating—three times each. To-and-fro friction, beginning well up on the neck, covering shoulders, back, and hips. Give three times.

2. Apply lubricant with long strokes up the spine, four rotary sweeps down the sides—twice.

3. Friction.

a. Heavy friction with the full hand down the spine—hands alternating each three times.

b. Heavy rotary, full sweep to the shoulders—three times.

c. From the shoulders down, across the arms, stroking toward the spine, following the ribs—six times.

d. Lower back, heavy friction upward over the buttocks toward the spine—three times. Upward on the hips—three times. Outward, using the thumb and the thenar surface over the crest of the ilium—three times.

4. Percussion up and down on the left side, the same on the right side. Give twice.

5. Stroking.

a. Full sweeps covering the back—three times.

b. Slow strokes with the full hand down the spine—six times.

Oil Rub—O. R. The oil rub softens the skin, and is frequently used as a protective after sweating treatments. It may be given in the same manner as the centripetal friction, omitting procedure number one, light friction, and procedure number four, percussion. If desired, the following abbreviated method may be used, always omitting the percussion after hot treatments:

GENERAL ORDER:

1. Apply lubricant.
2. Rotary friction.
3. Percussion.
4. Stroking (centripetal).

Arms

1. Apply lubricant; beginning at the hands, with a long stroke, go over the arm up to the shoulder—three times.

2. Beginning at the hand, apply a long stroke up to the shoulder, returning with alternate rotary movements, three each to shoulder, arm, elbow, forearm, wrist, and hand—three times.

3. Percussion up and down twice on external surface. Give the same on the inner surface. Six percussion strokes to the hand.

4. Finish with long strokes from shoulder to finger tip—three times.

Legs

1. Beginning at the foot, apply lubricant with long strokes up to the hip with both hands, covering the entire surface—three times.

2. Apply long strokes from foot to knee, returning with alternate rotary movements, three each to knee, calf, ankle, and foot—twice. Return to the hip with a long stroke. With hands on the anterior surface of the thigh, from hip to knee, give eight or ten rapid alternate rotary friction movements. Give the same on the posterior surface of the thigh —three times. Continue with rotary friction from the knee down as at first—once.

3. Percussion the same as for the arm.

4. Long stroking movement from hip to toes— three times.

Chest and Abdomen

1. Lubricate; with hands working together, begin at median line below, going lightly up the median line and down the sides—three times.

2. Hands working together, stroke the neck down-

ward three times, then give rotary movements three each, above clavicle, to shoulder, below clavicle, nine down each side, nine up over the median part of abdomen and chest—three times.

3. Have the patient take and hold a deep breath. Beginning well over at the lower left side, give percussion up that side to the top of the shoulder, down on the same side of the median line, up on the right side of the median line to the top of the shoulder, and down the right side—twice.

4. Stroking—movement the same as in lubricating—three times.

Back

Procedure the same as for the chest. Finish with six long, gentle, downward strokes to the spine.

Talcum Rub—Talc. R. The talcum rub is useful where oil is objectionable, as in warm weather, or where there is a tendency to too free perspiration after treatment. It dries rather than softens the skin. It is also useful in hives, and should be given after a prolonged cool bath. The procedure is the same as with the oil rub.

Dry Friction—D. F. The procedure for dry friction or the dry hand rub (d. h. r.) is the same as for the oil rub except that no lubricant is used. If it is given briskly with vigorous to-and-fro friction and followed by percussion, the effect is to quicken the circulation in the skin and warm the surface. The treatment also stimulates heat production.

Slow, heavy friction without percussion, as to the spine, the forehead, etc., is sedative.

BATHS

Various procedures more or less similar and commonly called baths are included under this head.

1. Partial Immersion Baths

Hand-and-Arm Bath. The hand and arm may be immersed in neutral, hot, or cold water, or the two latter alternately. For this purpose, employ a foot tub (better one of elliptical shape) with sufficient water to immerse the hand, and the forearm to the elbow, or including the elbow. Very deep pails may be used. When hot water is used, it should be as hot as can be borne. Immersion of the hands in cold water is useful in controlling epistaxis.

To give hot and cold immersion to an infected hand or arm (blood-poisoning), employ two pails or tubs,—one of the hottest water that can be borne, and the other of ice water with a block of ice in it. To the cold water may be added one fourth or one half dram of crystals of permanganate of potassium; and to the hot water, about five times this quantity of oxalic acid. Immerse the hand and the arm in hot water for one and one half to two minutes, then in the cold for fifteen to thirty seconds. Continue these alternations for twenty-five minutes to an hour, finishing with the cold. Hot water should be added to the tub as fast as can be borne. The procedure should be repeated from one to four times daily as indicated. Other parts of the body, as the foot, may be treated in a similar manner. Massage is strictly contraindicated in infected conditions.

Foot Bath—Ft. B. The foot bath is one of the most useful measures in hydrotherapy. Its chief use is as a preliminary or adjunct to other treatment. It may be given with the patient lying or sitting, and is sometimes given with the patient standing. Large pails may be used, but more conveniently, tubs of an elliptical shape about sixteen inches long and eight to ten inches deep.

If the foot bath is given in bed or on a treatment table, protect the bedding or the table coverings with an oilcloth. Protect the patient with a blanket or a sheet, covering the knees and the foot tub. Tuck this covering about the legs and the foot tub so as to prevent the circulation of air. When the feet are taken out of the water, dry them thoroughly, especially between the toes, and immediately cover well with dry coverings or put on slippers.

1. HOT FOOT BATH—H. FT. B. The water should rise above the ankles. The bath may be at a temperature of about 105° F., and should be gradually increased, as fast as can be borne, to a maximum of about 120° F. It may be continued from five minutes to half an hour. At the close, the feet should receive a pour or dash of cold water and be thoroughly dried.

It is often necessary to use the cold head compress if the bath is very hot, continued for a long time, or if given with the patient sitting up, and in all cases where there is a tendency to faintness.

Effects. The hot foot bath is an efficient means of securing a derivative effect. It draws blood from all other parts, especially those which are congested. The cold pour or douche given at the close helps to maintain the blood in the feet. It is sometimes desirable to use a *mustard foot bath,* in which case add three or four tablespoonfuls of mustard to the water.

2. COLD FOOT BATH—C. FT. B. The water should be from two to four inches deep, at a temperature of 45° to 60° F. The feet should be previously warmed, and during the bath, rubbed with the hands, or one foot by the other. Duration, one to five minutes.

Effects. The shallow cold foot bath causes reflex contraction of the blood vessels of the brain, the pelvic organs, and the liver; also contraction of the muscles of the uterus, the bladder, the stomach, and the intestines. The cold foot bath should not be given during the menstrual period, or in case of acute pulmonary, abdominal, or pelvic inflammation.

3. ALTERNATE HOT AND COLD FOOT BATH—H. & C. FT. B. Use two tubs of water deep enough to well cover the ankles, one as hot as can be borne (temperature gradually raised), and the other at 45° F. Immerse the feet in the hot water for two minutes, and in the cold fifteen to thirty seconds. Continue alternations for ten to fifteen minutes, wiping from the cold.

Effects. The alternate hot and cold foot bath produces powerful fluxion effects in the feet. For this reason, the derivation secured by its use is very decided and enduring. It is especially useful in congestive headache, in which case a cold compress should be applied to the head, or to the head and the neck at the same time. It is also useful in treating infections of the foot, Charcot's joint at the ankle, tuberculosis of the ankle or of the bones of the foot, and in gangrene to hasten the production of the line of demarcation.

Leg Bath—Lg. B. For the leg bath, a tub should be provided deep enough to immerse the legs to the knees. If used in the treatment room, the tub should be fitted with an outlet at the base, so as to obviate the necessity of tipping the tub over to empty it. It should be placed near or against the wall, so that it may be filled from a hot and a cold water faucet by two short rubber hose. Also provide a stool an inch or two higher than the tub.

The patient should be covered with a sheet or a blanket, and, if the room is not warm enough, a large fomentation cloth or Turkish towel placed over the knees. If necessary, place a doubled fomentation cloth under the knees, over the rim of the tub.

1. HOT LEG BATH—H. LG. B. Begin with the water at 103° F., and increase the temperature as rapidly as can be borne. Use cold cephalic and cervical compresses (or ice bags), renewing before they become warm. In case the leg bath is combined with other hot treatment, as fomentations to the spine, an ice bag over the heart may be necessary, especially if the treatment is continued to profuse perspiration. The treatment should be continued in a given case until the desired effect is produced. This may require from five to thirty minutes, according to conditions and the particular effect desired. Finish with a cold dash to the legs.

Effects. The hot leg bath is a much more powerful derivative measure than the hot foot bath, and is one of the best treatments that can be used for this purpose. When combined with fomentations to the spine or the chest, and especially when the patient drinks some hot liquid at the same time, very profuse perspiration is produced. If used in the home, such a sweating treatment should be concluded by a cold mitten friction; if given in the treatment room, by a graduated or alternate hot and cold shower and spray. The pail pour is also sometimes used for the same purpose.

2. ALTERNATE HOT AND COLD LEG BATH—H. & C. LG. B. The procedure is the same as with the alternate foot bath. A cold compress should be applied to the head and often an ice bag to the heart.

4—Hydrotherapy

Effects. The alternate hot and cold leg bath produces most powerful fluxion in the legs and the feet. It is especially useful in treating œdema of these parts, whether due to heart disease or to vascular disease. After two or three treatments have been given, pieces of ice should be added to the cold water. The treatment may be followed by heavy centripetal friction to the feet and the legs.

Sitz Bath—Z. For the sitz bath, a porcelain sitz tub with special inlet and outlet is the most satisfactory; one of metal or an ordinary washtub may be used. In addition, there should be a foot tub for immersion of the feet in hot water; also a pail of cold water with a hand towel for keeping the head cool.

Protect the patient from contact with the tub by towels or fomentation cloths placed behind the back and under the knees. Cover the patient with a blanket or a sheet. The temperature of the foot bath should be at least two or three degrees above that of the sitz bath.

1. COLD SITZ BATH—C. Z. Sufficient water should be used to cover the hips and come up on the abdomen. Temperature, 55° to 75° F. Foot bath, 105° to 110° F. Time, one to eight minutes. Rub the hips to promote reaction. Friction mitts may be used. If desired, the water may be flowing. It adds somewhat to the effect.

Effects. If of brief duration—two to four minutes—it greatly stimulates the pelvic circulation, and the musculature of the bowels, the bladder, and the uterus. When it is given with very cold water (55° to 65° F.) and vigorous friction (cold rubbing sitz bath), these effects are intensified. The cold rubbing sitz bath is very useful in constipation, in subinvolution, and in hastening the absorption of residual thickening after pelvic inflammations.

2. PROLONGED COLD SITZ BATH—C. Z. Temperature, 70° to 85° F. Time, fifteen to forty minutes. Foot bath, 105° to 110° F. This may be begun at a higher temperature, and very gradually lowered to the desired point (graduated sitz bath). It should not at any time cause chilliness, and rubbing is not desirable. If necessary to give a sensation of warmth, a fomentation or a wrapped spinal hot-water bottle may be applied to the spine.

Effects. The prolonged cold sitz bath causes extreme and lasting contraction of the pelvic blood vessels and of the muscular wall of the uterus. It is therefore very useful in subinvolution.

3. NEUTRAL SITZ BATH—NEUT. Z. Temperature, 92° to 97° F. Foot bath, 102° to 106° F. Apply cold compress to the head. Time, twenty minutes to one or two hours. Effect, sedative.

4. VERY HOT SITZ BATH—H. Z. Begin at a temperature of about 100° F., and rapidly increase to 106° to 115° F. Foot bath, 110° to 120° F. It should be kept at least two degrees hotter than the temperature of the sitz bath. Keep the head cool by cold cephalic and cervical compresses. Duration, three to eight minutes. At the close, cool the bath to neutral for one to three minutes. If sweating has been produced, pour cold water over the shoulders and the chest. The hot sitz bath is used to relieve dysmenorrhea, and pelvic pain from various other causes.

5. REVULSIVE SITZ BATH—REV. Z. Begin at a temperature of 100.° F., and increase rapidly to 106° to 115° F. Foot bath, 110° to 120° F. Keep

the head cool by cold cephalic and cervical compresses. Duration, three to eight minutes. Finish by a cold pail pour to the hips; temperature of the water, 55° to 65° F.

Effects. The revulsive sitz produces a fluxion effect in the surface and deep blood vessels. It is one of the most useful measures in treating chronic inflammatory conditions of the pelvic viscera, such as various forms of salpingitis, ovaritis, cellulitis.

6. ALTERNATE HOT AND COLD SITZ BATH—H. & C. Z. Provide two sitz tubs installed side by side. Fill one with hot water at a temperature of 106° to 115° F., and the other with cold water at 55° to 85° F. Foot baths, 105° to 115° F. Apply cold compresses to the head and the neck. The patient sits in the hot water for two or three minutes, then in the cold for fifteen to twenty seconds, and again in the hot water. Three complete changes from hot to cold are made, as is usual in alternate treatments.

Effects. The alternate sitz bath produces powerful fluxion effects in the pelvic viscera. It is useful in chronic pelvic inflammations after the patient has become accustomed to the revulsive sitz. It may also be used to great advantage in atonic constipation.

Hot Half Bath—H. ½ B. The hot half bath is given in a full-length bathtub. Fill the tub with water at 100° to 102° F., and deep enough to reach the patient's navel when the patient is sitting. The patient now sits down in the tub, with the shoulders covered by a sheet, and the head kept cool by a cold wet towel. It is usually best to apply this just before the patient enters the bath.

The temperature of the bath is gradually raised to 108° or 110° F., and continued for three to eight minutes. If necessary, an ice bag should be used over the heart. Conclude the treatment by a cold pail pour to the hips.

The effects and the uses are the same as those of the revulsive sitz. This treatment must not be confused with the shallow bath, which is given with cold water, and is a tonic measure.

2. Full Immersion Baths

The tub used for general or full immersion baths should be long enough that the body may be completely immersed,—a 6-foot tub for men; in many cases, a 5½-foot tub is long enough for women. The head should rest on an air pillow or a small invalid ring; and for emaciated patients, a folded sheet should be placed under the nates. In a hot bath, the head must be kept cool by a cold compress. In the case of full tub baths, it is especially necessary that the temperature of the water be tested by means of a thermometer. When tub baths are ordered, the desired temperature should be specified on the prescription.

Plain Tub Baths. 1. Hot Tub Bath—H. B. or H. Tub. Temperature, 100° to 106° F. Time, two to twenty minutes. Give cold water to drink freely. Keep the head cool. If necessary, apply an ice bag to the heart and the back of the neck. It is usually best to begin the bath at about 98°, gradually raising the temperature to the desired point. The treatment may be finished by cooling the bath, or by a cold pour or shower given immediately after the patient rises from the bath.

Effects. The effect varies according to the temperature and the duration of the bath. If it is much prolonged, or if the temperature is very high, profuse sweating is produced. The hot tub bath may be used as a preparation for cold treatment. A warm bath at 100° to 102° F. is very effective in relieving opisthotonos in tubercular meningitis, and is also beneficial in other diseases associated with spasticity of the muscles.

2. NEUTRAL BATH—NEUT. B. Temperature, 94° to 97° F. Time, fifteen minutes to three or four hours; usually twenty to thirty minutes. Wet the forehead and the face in cool water. Cool the bath two or three degrees just at the close. Dry the patient with a sheet directly from the bath. Use no percussion or unnecessary rubbing, as this destroys the sedative effect.

Effects. The neutral bath is given for sedative purposes. To accomplish this, it must exert a relaxing effect, and so equalize the circulation as to reduce the amount of blood in the brain and the spinal cord. Its temperature will therefore vary with the condition of the patient, especially as regards the skin temperature. The season of the year must also be taken into account. For these reasons, it may frequently be necessary to employ the upper limit of the neutral temperatures, or raise the bath to 98°, or even 99°. The air of the bathroom should be warm; and if the bath is much prolonged, stretch a sheet over the tub. The cooling of the water two or three degrees at the close is usually necessary to prevent the slight sensation of chilliness that is likely to be produced by contact with the air on emerging from the bath. When used for insomnia, it should be given just previous to retiring.

3. CONTINUOUS FLOWING BATH—CONT. FLOW. B. This requires a special tub six feet long, provided

with a large outflow and a large overflow vent near
the top. The inflow may consist of one large opening at the head of the tub, or of several small openings along the sides. The water is supplied directly
from a mixing chamber, which is fitted with a
thermometer. A continuous supply of hot water
at a constant temperature and pressure must be
assured, also of cold water. The water is regulated
to the desired temperature in the mixing chamber
before it is turned into the tub. The usual temperature is 98° F. When the tub is full and over-
flowing, the quantity is reduced to a gentle stream.
The patient rests on a canvas hammock that swings
from the rim of the tub. He is protected by a canvas cover, and provided with a rubber air pillow.
An ice turban should be placed upon his head, and
cold water should be given him plentifully to drink.
It is well to keep a bath thermometer in the tub,
and consult it frequently, not relying wholly upon
the thermometer in the mixing chamber.

As this bath is used chiefly in maniacal cases, the
patient must be watched constantly. A very excited or violent patient, before being placed in the
tub, should be wrapped in a sheet or blanket pack,
which must be securely pinned about him. The
duration of the bath depends upon the degree of
sedative effect obtained. It may last for hours
or days. In the latter case, the patient must be
removed once or twice in the twenty-four hours,
proper attention given to the bowels, and the skin
anointed with oil to prevent too great maceration.
The continuous flowing bath is perhaps the most
useful treatment in excited cases of insanity. It,
together with the wet sheet pack, has revolution-
ized the treatment of mania.

4. COLD BATH—C. B. or C. TUB. Temperature,
55° to 90° F. Time, a plunge only, to twenty or

more minutes, depending on the temperature and the effect desired. It is necessary to employ rubbing constantly or at frequent intervals. The patient's face should be bathed in cold water before he enters the bath, and it is imperative that the skin be warm before the bath is given.

Effects. When a cold bath is given to a patient with a normal temperature, and lasts for a few seconds or minutes only, the effect is that of a stimulant and a tonic. The *cold rubbing bath* is the most commonly employed method of treating typhoid fever in institutions where tubs are available and convenient to use. The strict Brand bath is too severe a measure for many patients. The methods of, indications for, and the precautions in the use of the cold bath have been very fully discussed in the author's texts for physicians and nurses.

5. BRAND BATH. As advised by Brand for the treatment of typhoid fever, the procedure is as follows:

Temperature, 65° to 70° F. Bathe the face and the head in cold water or ice water. Lift the patient into the bath. Rub constantly to keep the blood in the skin. If chilling cannot be prevented by vigorous rubbing, the patient must be removed from the bath. Time, fifteen minutes. Repeat when the temperature reaches 102.5° or 103° F. Effect, antipyretic.

6. GRADUATED BATH—GRAD. B. The graduated bath is as efficient in lowering febrile temperature when much prolonged, and is less objectionable to the patient than is the Brand bath. The patient should be made comfortable by an air pillow, and a hammock made by tying a sheet across the tub, fastening the corners and sides underneath. Tem-

perature—begin at 98° or above, depending on the height of the fever; that is, from three to five degrees lower than the mouth temperature. The skin must be warm to begin with. Apply cold compresses to the head. Gradually reduce the temperature of the bath to about 85° F., when below 90° F., or if the patient feels chilly or shows goose flesh, he should be rubbed constantly to keep the blood in the skin, and so prevent or overcome chilling. A spine bag filled with hot water may be laid along the spine for the same purpose. Both pulse and temperature should be closely watched during the bath. The temperature of the patient should be taken every twelve or fifteen minutes. On removal, immediately wrap the patient in a sheet, drying quickly; and if there is goose flesh or chilliness, rub briskly with the hands until the blood returns to the skin. If the patient is very cyanotic, put him into a hot blanket pack for a few minutes, and take him out with a cold mitten friction. Effect, tonic chiefly, or antipyretic, according to the condition in which it is given.

7. COLD SHALLOW BATH—C. S. B. Fill the tub four to six inches deep with water at 65° to 75° F. The patient's feet should be warm before he enters, and the head should be kept cool by cold wet towels. The patient sits down in the cold water and rubs the arms, the legs, and the chest vigorously while the attendant rubs the hips and the back. Cold water dipped from the tub is dashed over the shoulders and the back, and these parts are again rubbed. The patient now lies down in the bath and rubs the chest and the abdomen, while the attendant rubs the legs. This procedure may be repeated once or twice if desired.

The entire treatment should last from two to four minutes; and when the patient emerges from the bath, the skin surface should be in a decided glow, otherwise the proper effect has not been obtained. The cold shallow bath is one of the most vigorous tonic measures employed in hydrotherapy.

Hydroelectric Baths. The tub provided for these baths should be completely insulated by resting on a base of some insulating material. The mixing faucet should be attached to the wall over the foot of the tub and make no contact with the tub itself. The outlet should also be disconnected from the plumbing, the waste water running into a cement gutter. For the hydroelectric or electrothermal bath, a neutral temperature is usually employed. The patient's body and limbs are completely immersed in the water, the head lying on an air pillow, and kept cool by a cold wet towel. The electrodes should hang from the side of the tub, so they may be placed in any desired position along the sides or at the feet of the patient. The treatment is begun with one electrode at the feet and the other near the arm on the opposite side. The electricity is turned on to comfortable tolerance. Time, five to twenty minutes. After half the time has expired, the electrodes should be reversed, the one at the foot of the tub being brought up along the arm of the same side, and the one near the opposite arm being placed at the foot on the same side. These directions do not apply to the galvanic bath. When galvanism is used, the positive pole should be placed at the head, preferably dipping into the water underneath the pillow, and the negative pole at the feet.

Precautions. To avoid shock, have no current passing when the patient steps in or out. Be sure that all appliances are in good order before the patient enters the bath. Keep all parts of the generator, the switches, the rheostat, etc., absolutely dry and clean. Do not handle the switches or the rheostat with wet hands.

Do not start or stop the motor generator or turn the current on or off while the rheostat is turned on. After the patient enters the bath, the current switch is turned on and the motor or generator started; next gradually increase the current by turning the rheostat. Before the patient leaves the bath, turn off the current by reversing these steps; that is, first gradually lessen the current by turning down the rheostat, then stop the generator and turn off the switch.

1. FARADIC TUB BATH—NEUT. FARAD. The induction coil used should be large enough to supply amply any current strength needed, and the interrupter should be so arranged as to give any desired rate of vibration; at least, provision should be made for both slow and rapid interruptions.

Effects. Slow or medium faradic for five or six minutes is stimulating and tonic. It is beneficial in flaccid paralysis and in general atonic conditions of the muscular system. Rapid faradic, given with less current strength, and continued for twelve or fifteen minutes, is sedative. The faradic tub bath is less satisfactory than sinusoidal, as the alternations of the current are sharp and therefore less agreeable to the patient.

2. SINUSOIDAL TUB BATH—NEUT. SINU. For the production of a simple sinusoidal current the sinusoidal dynamo devised by Kellogg is the most satisfactory. There are many appliances for producing composite wave currents which are highly efficient and often very pleasing to the patient. These currents are fully illustrated in the author's text, ''Essentials of Medical Electricity.'' The

slow sinusoidal current gives a maximum muscular
contraction with a minimum of unpleasantness. The
contraction of the muscles is vigorous and painless.

Effects. The slow sinusoidal for five or six minutes is stimulating and tonic. Rapid sinusoidal for
a longer time is sedative. The slow sinusoidal is
useful in all forms of flaccid paralysis, atrophied
muscles, weak abdominal muscles, splanchnoptosis,
etc. It is much more agreeable to the patient, and
more efficient, than faradic electricity, and for
these reasons, should replace the faradic wherever
possible.

3. GALVANIC TUB BATH—NEUT. GALV. Unless
given from a battery of cells or a small dynamo
not connected with a lighting system, galvanic
electricity is dangerous. Even then burns may
result if it is carelessly used. Moreover, the effects
usually sought from the galvanic tub bath may be
obtained in other ways without risk to the patient.

Precautions. In the use of the galvanic tub
bath, all the precautions mentioned before should be
carefully observed. The current must never be
turned on before the patient enters, and must always be turned off before he steps from the bath.
If this is not done, a severe shock may be occasioned as the patient places one foot in the bath
with the other on a wet floor, thus making a
grounding contact through the cement floor, or
worse yet, through some metal pipe near.

Always ascertain the polarity before the electrodes are placed. To do this, place the electrodes
in water an inch or two apart, and turn the current
on. The bubbles formed at the negative pole are
larger and more numerous than those formed at the
positive pole. Place the positive pole at the head
of the tub, and the negative at the foot. Be sure

that they do not come in contact with the skin at any point. Sinusoidal and the secondary faradic are alternating currents, and there can therefore be no distinction as to polarity.

Effects. The positive pole is a vasoconstrictor, the negative pole a vasodilator. For this reason, the positive pole decreases congestion, the negative pole increases it. The positive pole has a sedative effect, the negative pole a stimulant or irritant effect. These are the reasons for placing the positive pole at the head and the negative pole at the feet of the patient. As a neutral temperature is used, the total effect is decidedly sedative. All forms of the electric tub bath are disagreeable to some persons.

The bath should last from ten to fifteen minutes, and from twenty to thirty-five milliamperes should be used. The amperage should not be high enough to produce an unpleasant sensation. If there are saline substances dissolved in the bath, the amperage will run much higher before the same effects are produced as with ordinary water. With thin subjects, a comparatively low amperage must be used; with subjects in good flesh or overweight, a stronger current may be employed.

Medicated Baths. A tub bath may be altered by the addition of various medicaments. Such baths are not of great practical importance except in a very limited number of skin diseases.

1. SALINE BATH—SAL. B. Add from three to five pounds of common salt to the tub of water at 90° to 94° F. Time, ten to twenty minutes. The addition of salt increases the tonic effect through stimulation of the peripheral circulation so that the water may be a few degrees cooler than an

ordinary neutral bath. The effect is similar to a
bath in sea water.

2. ALKALINE BATH—ALK. B. Add one half to
one pound of bicarbonate of soda to the tub of
water at neutral temperature. One fourth pound
of carbonate of soda may be used. Time, ten to
twenty minutes. Effects, relieves cutaneous irritation, itching, etc. Useful in certain skin diseases, as eczema and hives.

Nauheim Bath. The effervescent or artificial
Nauheim bath is one in which water is charged
with saline substances and carbon dioxide. Many
different formulas are used to prepare such a bath.
To produce the carbon dioxide in a bath, it is
necessary that an acid come in contact with an
alkaline carbonate, setting free the carbon dioxide;
or salines may be dissolved in the water, and the
carbon dioxide added from a generator. Various
proprietary mixtures prepared in cakes are offered
for use.

In using these, dissolve the sodium chloride and
the sodium bicarbonate in forty or fifty gallons of
water. The bottom of the tub is then covered with
rubber sheeting. On this rubber sheeting place
the acid cakes. In about three minutes, when effervescence is well under way, the patient should lie
down in the bath.

A very complete and satisfactory formula is the
following:

Sodium carbonate (sal soda) - - 1½ ℔s.
Sodium bicarbonate (baking soda) ½ ℔.
Calcium chloride - - - - - - 3 ℔s.
Sodium chloride (common salt) - 2 ℔s.
Sodium bisulphate - - - - - 1 ℔.

After mixing the first four, dissolve in a few
inches of warm water in the bottom of the bath

tub. When they are thoroughly dissolved, ˙ ˙˙
tub with water at the desired temperature
sodium bisulphate, which is the acid pa
formula, should be granular or pounded
dissolved separately in a wooden or paper ƿ..
taining hot water. As some time may be requ...d
for this to dissolve, it should be prepared before
the bath is to be given. When thoroughly dissolved, pour into the tub, and quickly mix with
the rest of the water. The bath is now ready for
use. The amounts of the saline ingredients may
be gradually increased for the succeeding baths of
a course.

Three fourths of a pound of commercial hydro-
chloric acid may be used instead of the sodium
bisulphate. This should be mixed with two or
three times its volume of water, and after the salts
are all dissolved and the tub is filled with water
at the desired temperature, the bottle containing
the acid should be opened under water. It may be
moved about to hasten the diffusion of the acid
into the water of the bath.

The following is a simpler and less expensive
formula, and is the one we usually employ:

Sodium chloride   - - - -   3 to 8 ℔s.
Sodium bicarbonate - - -   ¾ to 1½ ℔s.
Sodium bisulphate (commercial) - - 1 ℔.

The temperature of the bath should range from
85° to 94° F. The lower temperatures should be
used for the later baths of a series. The duration
of the bath should at first be from five to eight
minutes. The time may then be gradually extended
to fifteen or even twenty minutes. A cold compress should be applied to the head, and an ice bag
to the heart. The patient should not be rubbed
during the bath. About three baths a week may

taken for three or four weeks. Not over twenty baths should constitute a course.

Effects and Therapeutic Use. The effects of the bath are due to the cutaneous stimulation of the vasomotors produced by the carbon dioxide and salines dissolved in the water. The peripheral heart is stimulated, and the cutaneous circulation is greatly hastened. The heart beats slower and with greater ease. In normal individuals, there may be a fall of ten to fifteen beats in the pulse rate following a single bath; while in case of a very rapid pulse, the decrease may reach as high as twenty-five to forty beats a minute. Examination of the heart after the bath in cases of a valvular lesion or cardiac dilatation shows a stronger, steadier beat; the rhythm becomes regular, the sounds become clearer, and certain murmurs may disappear entirely. The pulse becomes full, and blood pressure rises 20 or 30 mm. The area of dullness of an enlarged, dilated heart is often lessened one half inch or more all around its border. Both the systole and the diastole are lengthened.

The Nauheim bath also stimulates metabolism, and hastens the elimination of gouty toxins. It exerts a beneficial effect upon nutrition, and is therefore of much use in diseases of metabolism.

If a course of baths is continued too long, overstimulation results, passive dilatation of the blood vessels occurs, the heart beats with less force, the rhythm is disturbed, and there will be palpitation. This may be prevented by keeping the duration of the bath well within fifteen minutes, stopping short of the maximum number of baths that may be used in one course, and using the ice bag over the heart during the treatment.

Oxygen Bath—O_2B. This bath is similar in effect and technique to the Nauheim bath. It was introduced by Sarason of Berlin in 1904. Instead of carbon dioxide, the bath water is charged with oxygen gas. To produce this requires the action of a catalyzer upon an oxygen-containing chemical. Oxygen generators are also used for the same purpose, but are not regarded as so efficient, because of the larger size of the bubbles. It is the oxygen that is dissolved in the water which produces the results, rather than that which collects as bubbles producing effervescence.

The standard method of preparing the oxygen bath is as follows: Fill the tub with sufficient water, at 95° to 98° F., to cover the patient to his neck. Dissolve in this 300 grams of sodium perborate ($NaBO_3$) by sprinkling uniformly over the surface of the water. Next add the catalyzer, 15 grams of manganese borate ($Mn_3(BO_3)_2$) by the same procedure. The patient gets into the water in one or two minutes after the catalyzer has been put in. The liberation of oxygen continues for fifteen to twenty minutes. The patient should remain as quiet as possible, moving the limbs only occasionally. The sensation is that of an agreeable tickling and prickling about the spine, the shoulders, and the limbs. At the end of twenty minutes, remove the patient, and dry with as little disturbance as possible. If a brownish sediment remains in the tub, it may easily be rinsed off, if this is done immediately after the bath.

The baths may be administered on alternate days or for four or five days a week, a course consisting of twenty to thirty baths. The effects are similar to those of the carbon dioxide bath in the production of a powerful stimulation of the peripheral blood vessels. The oxygen bath, however, differs essentially in the following points: Instead of the redness of the skin produced by the carbon dioxide

5—Hydrotherapy

bath, there is either no change, or the skin is paler, the peripheral diversion of blood occurring into the skeletal muscles rather than the skin. A lowering of blood pressure occurs after the oxygen bath, instead of a rise, as after the carbon dioxide bath. For this reason, it is indicated in cases of high blood pressure and in cardiac and renal diseases associated with increased vascular tension.

It is also a powerful sedative to the nervous system, and is therefore a most efficient measure in the treatment of insomnia, also in asthma, neurasthenia, and various paræsthesias. Because of the tendency to paleness of the skin, it is an advantage to precede the bath by some heating procedure, such as a hot foot bath, fomentations to the spine, or a short electric light bath. For the same reasons, the bath is administered at higher temperatures than the carbon dioxide bath. For sedative purposes, the bath should be administered in the afternoon or the early evening, or at least an hour before retiring. In cases of hypertension, reductions in blood pressure of from fifteen to thirty-five mm. Hg. have been reported.

3. Miscellaneous

Russian Bath. The Russian bath consists in the immersion of the body in hot vapor. The steam, as it is turned into the Russian room, partially condenses, and hangs suspended as a thick fog. For every gram of steam that thus condenses, 537 calories of heat are liberated. This fact accounts for the intense heating effect obtained by the use of this form of hot treatment.

For the Russian bath, provide a steam-tight room with a marble slab. A sliding window should be so arranged at the end of the slab that the patient's head may be outside the steam room. The steam should enter below the slab, so as not to strike the patient directly, and be controlled by a valve near the sliding window, so that the attendant may regu· late the amount of steam; at the same time, keep the head cool by frequently changed cold compresses to the head and the neck.

· *Procedure.* Move the bowels by an enema, and give a preliminary hot foot bath. Have the patient drink water before and frequently during the bath. This is necessary in order to provide for the profuse perspiration that the treatment should induce. See that the slab is warm; if not, pour over it several pails of hot water. Warm the room to about 100° F., and cover the slab with a folded sheet.

The patient is now assisted onto the table, and lies on the back, with the head on an air pillow just outside the opening. The window is lowered, and a towel wrung from ice water is placed about the neck, or hung across the lower end of the window and tucked around the neck. Another cold compress is applied to the head, and covers the temporal arteries. A third cold compress should be applied to the precordia. In some cases, it will be necessary to use an ice bag over the heart.

Next turn on the steam, gradually raising the temperature of the room to 115° or 120° F. A small amount of steam should be constantly escaping to maintain the temperature. Change the compresses to the head and the neck frequently. The patient should be closely watched during the entire time of the treatment. The bath should last from ten to thirty minutes. Just before the patient rises from the slab, renew the ice compress to the head. Finish the treatment with a graduated or alternate spray or shower, or better still, a shampoo and a graduated shower. The spray or shower should be in the Russian room or only a few steps from it.

Effects. The effects of vigorous sweating measures have been considered elsewhere. The "washing out" effect is, perhaps, the greatest; and the thoroughness of this depends very largely upon the water taken before and during the treatment. Sweating measures greatly increase katabolism, especially of carbohydrates and fats. The products of nitrogenous metabolism show more complete oxidation.

The Russian bath is of great service in obesity, chronic rheumatism with obesity, gout, Bright's disease, auto-intoxications, chronic alcoholism, and in arteriosclerosis unless extreme. It is contraindicated in diabetes, valvular heart disease, all diseases associated with emaciation, and in extreme arteriosclerosis.

Cabinet Vapor Bath. The principle involved in the cabinet vapor bath is the same as that of the Russian bath. Various waterproof cabinets are offered for sale. They are useful in a home where more elaborate facilities cannot be provided. An alcohol stove heats water in a basin under or near the stool provided for the patient. This is continued until the cabinet is full of vapor, when it is ready to enter. The patient sits on the stool, with the head outside the cabinet. The duration of the treatment should depend upon the rapidity of vaporization and upon the effect desired. The preliminaries, procedure, and precautions to be taken are the same as in the Russian bath. Conclude the treatment with a shampoo, a cold towel rub, a graduated shower, or other cold application.

Turkish Bath. The Turkish bath consists in the immersion of the body in hot air. The Russian room may be used for this purpose, and conveniently heated by steam coils. The patient is treated in the same manner as in the Russian bath. The head and the neck should be kept cool by cold compresses, and, if necessary, an ice bag should be applied over the heart. The temperature of the room should be gradually raised from 120° to about 170°_F. The bath may last from fifteen to forty-five minutes. Perspiration is often somewhat delayed, in which case brisk friction to the skin may hasten its appearance. If perspiration is much delayed, the patient is likely to behave badly in the hot air bath, and for this reason, should be closely watched until free perspiration is established. Owing to the difficulty with which some patients react to dry hot air, the applicability of the♦ Turkish bath is somewhat more limited than that of the Russian bath.

Superheated Air Bath. In the superheated air bath, the temperature reaches 250° to 350° F. Special metal cabinets for the entire body or various parts may be purchased. The body or part to be treated should be thoroughly wrapped in Turkish toweling, and should not rest on any part of the cabinet likely to become hot enough to burn. By means of a gasoline or other burner, the temperature of the air in the cabinet is gradually raised to 250° or 350° F. These burners are placed just below the cabinet; over them are fitted inverted funnels with a short, wide stem leading directly into the cabinet. The entering hot air should be spread by means of an asbestos shield so that it will not directly strike the skin surface. The patient's pulse and general condition must be watched very closely during a full hot air bath. An ice bag should be kept on the heart, and ice compresses on the head and the neck. These precautions are not so necessary where only a single part, such as a knee or a foot and an ankle, is being treated. The treatment may be concluded by an alcohol or witch-hazel rub. Great care must be exercised that the patient does not take cold afterward.

The Turkish toweling with which the body or the limb is wrapped quickly absorbs the perspiration, thus preventing its collecting on the skin in drops. Should it collect in drops, burning is more likely to result.

Effects. The superheated air bath is a much more vigorous measure than the Turkish bath. It is of special advantage in articular rheumatism, whether occurring in acute rheumatic fever, chronic gouty rheumatism, or in specific arthritis. Where one or two joints are treated, the application should continue from twenty minutes to an hour after the temperature has reached 300° to 350° F. When the part is taken out, a momentary dash of cold water may be given, or the part may be cleansed from perspiration, and a heating compress applied.

Electric Light Bath—E. L. B. In giving the electric light bath, special upright or reclining cabinets fitted with mirrors and incandescent lights are used.

The feet should be warmed beforehand, or with the upright cabinet, a hot foot bath should be used. Cover the stool with a folded Turkish towel. Turn on the desired number of lights. When the cabinet is warmed, have the patient enter. Then close the cabinet, and apply a cold wet towel to the head and the neck. Renew this frequently. If there is a tendency to faintness or rapid pulse, use an ice bag to the heart as well. If a horizontal cabinet is used, cover the table with a folded sheet. Warm the cabinet, and place a rubber pillow for the patient's head. The patient then lies down, and is rolled into the cabinet, or the top is lowered, according to the style of cabinet used. The patient's head should be kept cool by cold compresses. There is less tendency to fainting with the horizontal than with the upright cabinet. The patient must be watched very carefully and constantly in order to guard against fainting. As he leaves the cabinet, a blanket or a sheet should be thrown about him if he is to go more than a few steps for the next part of the treatment. Finish with a spray or a shampoo and a spray. Where only general tonic effects are desired, the electric light bath should last from three to five or six minutes; for profuse sweating and eliminative effects, continue it from ten to eighteen or twenty minutes.

The air of the cabinet is not warmed to the same extent as the skin of the patient, since the heat is in the form of *radiant* energy. In this particular, the electric light bath differs essentially from the Russian or the Turkish bath, and from the effect produced by hot applications applied directly to the skin. This means that the heat of the electric light is not communicated to the body by direct conduction or by convection, but by the absorption of the rays of radiant energy, as they are retarded and stopped by the skin and subcutaneous tissues.

On the other hand, for strong derivative effects, the electric light bath is unsatisfactory. For derivative purposes, the heat must be brought in actual contact with the skin by the application of heated substance directly to the skin. For this reason, stronger derivative effects are secured by partial or full hot baths and hot packs.

SHAMPOOS

Swedish Shampoo—Ssh. For giving the Swedish or slab shampoo, provide a pail of water at

103° to 105° F., on a stool of convenient height near the head of the slab, also a shampoo brush and a half bar of soap. If the slab is not kept warm by being in a warm room, pour over it two or three pails, of hot water. Cover the slab with a doubled sheet, and assist the patient onto the slab, placing the head on an air pillow. Quickly lather an arm by dipping the brush and the soap into the pail of hot water and rubbing together over the part. With brisk, short movements, go over the part thoroughly, using as much friction as is comfortably borne. Do the same with the chest, the abdomen, and the legs.

Next assist the patient to turn over on the slab, by putting one arm under the neck and grasping the opposite shoulder, and the other arm under the near leg and grasping the opposite knee. Treat the back, the hips, and the backs of the legs in the same manner as the front of the body. Pour the remaining water in the pail over the patient to rinse off the soapsuds. Follow the shampoo by a warm and cold shower, spray, or pail pour.

Tub Shampoo—Tub Sh. Fill a bathtub with water at 98° F. The patient may sit on a wooden stool in the tub, or, if likely to chill, he should lie down in the tub, with the water deep enough to cover the chest. If the treatment is to be given with the patient sitting on a stool, treat first the arms, then the back, the chest, the abdomen, and the legs. If it is to be given with the patient immersed, raise one part at a time above the water, and proceed as usual, having the patient sit for the back and the chest. Finish by complete immersion in the tub, followed by a cold pail pour or shower.

Turkish Shampoo—Tur. Sh. The Turkish shampoo is given after sweating baths, such as the

Turkish, the Russian, or the electric light bath. The shampoo proper is preceded by manipulations and heavy friction to loosen the outer epidermis (so-called dead skin). It is the most thorough cleansing measure used.

1. Articles Necessary. Two pails of water at 90° F., one at 100° to 105° F., a loofah or shampoo brush, soap, two Turkish toweling mitts, two sheets, and two towels. In treating women, protect the hair by a rubber cap.

2. Procedure. If the sweating bath has not been taken in the shampoo room, the room must be well heated, and the slab warmed by pails of hot water poured over it. Cover with a doubled sheet, and assist the patient onto the slab. Place an air pillow under the head.

Manual Rubbing. Wet the face with water at 90° F. With the hands, dash water over every part separately, using long strokes and quickly covering the body. Beginning with the neck, about the ears, the hair, the forehead, over the nose and the chin, rub until the dead skin is thoroughly loosened. Wash off the loosened epidermis, dipping the hands frequently. For the chest and the abdomen, after applying the water, use transverse wringing and re-enforced rubbing, covering each part several times. Then wash off with water. For the arms, use spiral friction and wringing. For the legs, the same; with the thumbs, rub well about the ankles, the soles of the feet, the knees, etc. Turn the patient, and proceed with the back in the same manner as with the chest, also the thighs and the legs. Wash off the entire surface with water.

Friction Mitt. Dip the mitt into the second pail of water at 90° F., and beginning with the back and the backs of thighs and legs, go over each part twice, rubbing all thoroughly. Then turn the patient, and treat the chest, the abdomen, the arms, and the legs in the same manner. Wash off with the rest of the pail of water at 90° F.

Shampoo. Treat each **part** as in the Swedish shampoo, using hands, a loofah or bath brush, and the pail of water at 105° F.

Finish with a prolonged tepid or cool shower or spray, and at the close, a short cold spray. Dry thoroughly with sheets and towels. The patient should be careful not to take cold afterward.

PACKS

Packs are procedures in which a considerable portion of the body is enveloped in wet sheets or blankets for therapeutic purposes.

1. Hot Blanket Packs

The hot blanket pack is a procedure in which hot blankets are used to communicate heat to the body.

Full Hot Blanket Pack—H. B. P. *1. Articles Necessary.* Two double blankets or one single and one double blanket; one hot-water bottle and three spine bags half filled with hot water at 160° F.; a bowl or pail of ice water, with compresses for the head, the neck, and the heart; two Turkish towels; a tumbler, a drinking tube, and a pitcher of hot water for drinking.

2. Preliminaries. Move the bowels by an enema, give a hot foot bath, and have the patient drink hot water.

3. Procedure. Spread a double blanket on the treatment table or the bed. Adjust a cold compress to the patient's head while his feet are still in the hot foot bath. Fold the single blanket or another double blanket (the latter holds the heat longer) lengthwise in convenient width for passing through a wringer or wringing by hand. Wring from boiling water, quickly unfold and spread out over the dry blanket on the table.

Assist the patient to lie on the hot blanket, or if he is a bed patient, lift him onto the blanket. As quickly as possible, or as rapidly as can be borne, envelop the entire body except the head in the hot blanket. Place one spine bag between the legs, with one thickness of dry blanket between it and the moist blanket, and the hot-water bottle at the feet. The other spine bags should be placed along the sides of the trunk, in the same way as the one to the legs. Tuck both the wet and the dry blanket in well, especially at the feet and about the shoulders and the neck, so as to exclude the air. See that the wet blanket comes in contact with the body over its entire surface, so that no air spaces will be left.

Place cold compresses to the head and the neck, and protect the chin from the hot blanket by a soft dry towel. Renew the compresses before they are warmed to any extent.

For general sweating effects, a dry blanket may be placed between the patient and the wet blanket; but for strong derivative effects, the wet blanket should come in immediate contact with the skin.

The patient should perspire in a short time. If perspiration does not begin in about ten minutes, give hot water to drink, or a hot foot bath, or both. In giving the hot foot bath, let the blankets fall loosely about the tub, so as to prevent the circulation of air,

Continue the pack from twenty to thirty minutes; that is, until it ceases to have a heating effect. For tonic effects, it should be limited to five to ten minutes. Take the patient out by a cold mitten friction or a cold towel rub, removing the blanket from one part at a time, and covering with a dry blanket or bedding immediately after. It is usually most convenient to give the friction to the arms first, then to the chest and the abdomen, and to the legs last, giving the cold friction to the back after the wet blanket has been entirely removed.

4. Precautions. To much water left in the pack makes it feel very hot at first, but it cools more rapidly than when wrung nearly dry. For this reason, the pack should be wrung as dry as possible.

If the hot-water bags are too near the patient (not sufficiently covered), there is danger that burns will result. If complaint is made, the bags should at once be covered more thoroughly.

In some cases, it is necessary to use a cold compress or an ice bag to the heart.

General free perspiration should be induced by the pack. Long continued heat without perspiration results in harm.

In giving packs in case of paralyzed sensation or unconsciousness, during or soon after anæsthesia, in diabetes, dropsy, or insanity, a thickness of dry blanket should intervene between the patient and the wet blanket. Hot-water bottles should be more thoroughly covered, and the water used in them should be at a lower temperature, than ordinary.

5. Effects. The hot blanket pack is a vigorous sweating measure. It also produces decided derivation. Any sweating treatment decreases internal congestion, but this action is much more marked when the wet blanket is placed next to the skin. Where the congestion is not localized in some particular part, but consists of a general internal congestion, a general sweating treatment is usually sufficient for its relief. This is the case in the first stage of many fevers, in colds, grippe, etc.

In uræmia, eclampsia, and acute Bright's disease, both sudorific and strong derivative effects should be secured. In other forms of renal congestion, this is also necessary. In kidney insufficiency, the skin excretes much larger quantities of poison than in health. Free or profuse perspiration greatly aids in this vicarious function. This effect is not, however, the only nor the most important effect of sweating measures. The congestion of the skin secured by a hot pack reduces the congestion and high blood pressure in the kidney, and it soon begins to functionate when these are removed. The hot blanket pack is also useful in pneumonia and sometimes in typhoid fever. It is almost indispensable in the treatment of renal colic and gallstone colic. In these conditions, the pain is decreased immediately the pack is applied. In some cases, it entirely obviates the necessity for morphine; while in others, the dose may be cut to one third or one fourth the amount that would otherwise be required.

Dry Blanket Pack—D. B. P. Sweating may be produced by enveloping the body in a dry woolen blanket, and using hot-water bottles in the same way as with the wet pack. The same preliminaries should be observed, especially the giving of the hot foot bath before. It is quite essential that the patient take a considerable quantity of a hot drink during the treatment. Hot lemonade is ideal, as it favors both diaphoresis and diuresis. The sweating may be as profuse as with the wet pack, but the derivation is less efficient. Since no wet blanket is used, the patient may be first wrapped in a dry sheet and then in the dry blanket. The perspiration will be absorbed by the sheet; and so, in a short time, the effect will somewhat approach that of the sweating wet sheet pack.

Hot Trunk Pack—H. Tr. Pk. The method of applying the hot trunk pack is the same as with the full blanket pack. The wet blanket should include the pelvis but exclude the arms, reaching up to the axillæ. The outside dry blanket should include the whole body, but be used only for protection; it should not be wrapped tightly about the patient. A large dry fomentation cloth may well be applied between the patient and the wet blanket. Place a hot-water bottle over the abdomen, between the folds of the dry blanket, and spine bags on either side of the trunk. A hot foot bath should begin before and continue during the pack. Time, twenty to thirty minutes. If given for the relief of the pain of any form of colic, omit the cold friction at the close.

The hot trunk pack has the same general effect as the hot blanket pack. Since it covers less surface, the derivative effects are less. It is especially useful in digestive disturbances and in relieving the pain of renal and biliary colic, also in intestinal colic.

Revulsive Trunk Pack—Rev. Tr. Pk. The revulsive trunk pack consists of a hot trunk pack, given as directed above, and followed by a wet sheet trunk pack. Only this one change from heat to cold is made. The wet sheet is wrung from water at about 60° F., and applied to the trunk after the removal of the wet flannel blanket. The method is described under the heading of "Wet Sheet Packs."

The hot blanket should be removed while it is still hot, and the wet sheet applied at once, in much the same manner as for the revulsive compress.

The wet sheet trunk pack should remain in place until the heating stage is reached, when it may be removed, and a cold mitten friction or an alternate hot and cold spray douche given to the parts covered by the pack, followed by the same to the feet. If desired, the wet sheet trunk pack may be made a hot and heating trunk pack by inserting a hot-water coil or a hot-water bottle over the stomach.

The revulsive trunk pack is used for tonic purposes, also in chronic congestions of the liver and other digestive organs.

Hot Pelvic Pack—H. Pelv. Pk. The hot pelvic pack is applied in the same manner as the hot trunk pack. It should come well above the crests of the ilia and include nearly half of the thighs. It is useful in the relief of pelvic pain from dysmenorrhea, cystitis, proctitis, etc. Its effects do not greatly differ from those of the hot sitz bath, or large, very hot fomentations to the pelvis, both of which treatments are much easier to apply.

Revulsive Pelvic Pack—Rev. Pelv. Pk. This treatment is applied in the same way as the revulsive trunk pack. The cold pack should be prolonged to the heating stage. The effects are somewhat similar to those of the revulsive sitz and the hot half bath. It is useful in chronic congestions and chronic inflammations of the pelvic organs.

Hot Hip-and-Leg Pack—H. Hp. & Lg. Pk. The hip-and-leg pack should include the feet, the legs, the thighs, and the pelvis, reaching slightly above the crests of the ilia. A hot-water bottle should be placed at the feet, within the folds of the dry blanket; and a spine bag between the legs. Time, twenty to forty minutes. Taking one limb out at a time, finish with a cold mitten friction, to retain the blood in the limbs, thus maintaining the derivation secured by the hot pack.

Effects. The hot hip-and-leg pack is one of the most efficient derivative measures used in hydrotherapy. It is indicated in a large number of conditions, and when combined with the use of an ice bag over the congested part, is especially useful in depleting acutely inflamed organs. (See "Hot Packs with Ice Bags.")

Hot Leg Pack—H. Lg. Pk. The hot leg pack should include the feet, the legs, the knees, and half or more of the thighs. Hot-water bottles are used the same as above. Conclude the treatment in the same way.

The leg pack is somewhat less effective than the hip-and-leg pack. It is used for the same purposes, and is convenient where the pelvis cannot well be moved in giving treatment. A large fomentation may be used over the anterior surface and the sides of the pelvis at the same time, so as to cover nearly as much surface as the hip-and-leg pack.

Hot Packs with Ice Bags. Hot packs with the use of ice bags or the ice water coil are the most powerful and efficient derivative measures known to hydrotherapy. They are especially useful in reducing internal congestions, reducing or aborting local inflammation of deep parts, and relieving the pain incident to the inflammatory process. For these purposes, they are used only in the acute stage of the inflammatory process. The effects have been fully discussed in the more complete texts, in the consideration of inflammation and antiphlogistic effects.

The hot pack depletes the congested part by *drawing* the blood away to establish a collateral hyperæmia (pull effect), while the ice bag *drives* the blood away by reflexly stimulating prolonged and extreme contraction of the deep vessels of the inflamed part (push effect). The cold mitten friction given at the close causes retention of the blood in the skin by changing the passive hyperæmia to an active arterial hyperæmia.

These treatments are sometimes termed hot and cold packs; but this designation may cause confusion with the revulsive pack, in which case a cold (heating) wet sheet pack follows the hot blanket pack.

Ice bags may be used with the full pack or with any of the partial packs. The following combinations are useful in the acute stages of the diseases indicated:

APPENDICITIS—Hot hip-and-leg pack, with ice bag to the appendicial region.

PERITONITIS—Hot hip-and-leg pack, or leg pack only, with an ice compress or an ice cap to the abdomen.

PUERPERAL INFECTIONS AND ACUTE SALPINGITIS —Full hot blanket pack, or hip-and-leg pack, with ice to pelvis (suprapubic region).

MENINGITIS—Hot leg pack, with ice cravat, ice cap, and ice bag to base of brain and upper spine.

MASTOIDITIS—Hot hip-and-leg pack or full blanket pack, with ice cravat or ice bag over the carotid artery, ice cap to head, and fomentations to mastoid.

ALVEOLAR ABSCESS—Same as mastoiditis, except give fomentations to the jaw.

RENAL CONGESTION—Hot trunk pack or full blanket pack, with ice bag to the lower third of the sternum.

Other combinations will suggest themselves to the resourceful mind.

6—Hydrotherapy

Electrothermal Pack—Elec. Pk. The electrothermal pack consists of a specially prepared blanket containing flexible resistance wire. If it is to be used dry, the body or part to be treated should be wrapped in a dry sheet or a thin flannel blanket, and then in the electric blanket, and the electricity turned on. The amount of heat and the consequent effect may be governed by the strength of the current. If it is to be used wet, wrap the patient in a sheet wrung nearly dry from cold or tepid water, and then in the electric blanket. The treatment is concluded by a cold mitten friction, spray, or douche.

Effects. While the heat is not as intense with the electric blanket as with a blanket wrung from boiling water, it is a gradually increasing heat, hence more desirable for some purposes. It is useful for general sweating effects; and for this purpose, it may be used with or without the wet sheet. The dry pack may be used where mild continuous heat is desired, as after an operation. In this case, it should usually be applied only to the pelvis and the legs. A Turkish towel should be placed so as to form a pad under the heels, and then folded over the toes. All bony prominences should be similarly covered. The electric blanket may be used to reënforce other packs, and thus increase or prolong the effects.

The electric blanket should not be folded sharply at any place, as the wires are likely to be broken.

2. Wet Sheet Packs

A wet sheet pack is a procedure in which the body is wrapped in a wet sheet, outside of which is a dry blanket covering designed to regulate the evaporation.

Full Wet Sheet Pack—W. S. P. *1. Articles Necessary.* Two blankets, a sheet, a large hand towel, a Turkish towel, a pail of water at 60° to 70° F., a hot-water bottle.

2. Preliminaries. The feet and the entire body must be warm before the pack is applied. Chilliness, cold skin, or cyanosis are contraindications. In case the skin is not warm, a hot blanket pack or some other general hot treatment should be given. The head should be cooled by cold compresses before the patient enters the pack.

3. Procedure. Place a double blanket lengthwise of the treatment table, with the edge opposite the attendant hanging farther over the edge of the table than the near edge. The upper end should be about eight inches from the head of the table, and cover the lower third of the pillow. Wring the sheet as dry as possible from cold water, and spread out upon the blanket, so that its upper end will be a little below the upper end of the blanket. The patient then lies down upon the wet sheet, with the shoulders three or four inches below the upper edge. Both arms should be raised, while one side of the sheet is quickly wrapped around the body, drawn tightly in contact at all places, and the edge tucked under the opposite side. Below the hips, the sheet is wrapped around the leg of the same side. The arms are then lowered, and the opposite side of the sheet is drawn tightly over the body and tucked in. The sheet is folded over the shoulders and across the neck. The narrower edge of the blanket is drawn tightly around the body and tucked in along the side. The wider edge is disposed of in a similar manner, being pulled tightly to bring all parts in close contact, and the extra amount is wrapped entirely around the patient. The foot end is doubled under the feet. A Turkish

towel is placed about the neck, to protect the face
and the neck from contact with the blanket, and
more perfectly to exclude the air. An additional
blanket may be laid over the patient and tucked in
along the sides and about the feet, or two blankets
may be placed on the table at first.

4. Precautions. The wet sheet must come in
close contact with the body at all points. The dry
blanket must effectually prevent the entrance of
air, otherwise chilling will result. ''Warming up''
should occur promptly. The feet must be kept
warm during the entire treatment. It is permis-
sible to place a hot-water bottle to the feet to
hasten reaction in case this is delayed.

5. Stages. According to the degree of warming
the pack undergoes, it passes through four stages;
namely, *cooling or evaporating, neutral, heating, and
sweating.* It is often desirable to prolong the effect
of one stage, so that this effect may predominate.
Accordingly, the treatment is varied as follows:

1. COOLING OR EVAPORATING WET SHEET PACK—
EVAP. W. S. P. This is the first stage of the pack,
before the sheet has been warmed to the temperature of the body. To accomplish this requires from
five to twelve minutes. If, at the end of this time,
the sheet is removed and another applied, the effect
is intensified; or the blanket may be folded back,
and cold water sprinkled on the patient, over the
wet sheet. In the case of vigorous patients, the
dry coverings may be omitted entirely, considerable
water left in the sheet, and the patient fanned to
hasten evaporation, more water being sprinkled on
the sheet as soon as it is warmed slightly.

Effects. The evaporating wet sheet pack is a
powerful antipyretic measure. It is useful in
typhoid fevers, and in other continued fevers where

repeated antipyresis is necessary. Usually the pack should not be removed for renewal, but more cold water should be sprinkled on. As in the use of the cold tub bath in typhoid fever, rubbing is necessary if the water is very cold or the sheet sprinkled frequently. This is known as the *rubbing wet sheet pack*. Percussion should not be used. The greater the amount of water applied to the body, the stronger are the antipyretic effects, and consequently the quicker is the temperature of the patient reduced.

If desirable, the sheet may be wrung from hot water, the coverings being omitted. This is called a *hot evaporating sheet*. It is useful where slight chilliness exists. This treatment is not only antipyretic, but also lessens heat production, because of the initial heat and the consequent atonic reaction.

2. NEUTRAL WET SHEET PACK—NEUT. W. S. P. The neutral stage begins when the temperature of the pack reaches or slightly exceeds the temperature of the skin; that is, about 94° F. It may be prolonged by removing all but one or two dry coverings after the warming up has well begun. This allows sufficient evaporation to prevent the accumulation of heat above the temperature of the body. The protection must be uniform, and the entrance and circulation of air prevented.

Effects. The effects of the neutral wet sheet pack have been considered under the treatment of insomnia. A neutral temperature is secured the same as in the neutral bath. The marked sedative effects of the neutral pack are due more to the derivation secured than to the neutral temperature. In normal sleep, there is a lessening of the amount of blood in the brain, and a local decrease of blood pressure. The neutral pack brings about these changes, and thus aids in inducing relaxation and sleep.

If the pack is removed before sleep is produced, uncover one part at a time, drying thoroughly, and wrapping in a warm dry sheet; or entirely remove the pack, and immediately wrap the patient in a warmed sheet, finishing the drying as quickly as possible.

If the pack is removed after the patient has slept, conclude the treatment by a wet hand rub or a cold mitten friction, according to the degree of tonic effect desired.

The neutral wet sheet pack is also of use in the delirium of fevers, in mania, epilepsy, chorea, infantile convulsions, etc.

3. HEATING WET SHEET PACK—HEAT. W. S. P. The heating stage begins when the warming of the pack raises the skin temperature slightly above its usual degree; it ends at the beginning of general perspiration, which marks the establishment of a full reaction. For tonic effects, the pack should continue about twenty minutes. When the stage of a pack is not prescribed, this treatment is intended.

Effects. Tonic and heating effects are secured by it. These may be prolonged by applying cold water to the head and the neck continuously, so as to check extreme sweating. The chief effect of the heating wet sheet pack is the production of derivation. The reaction and the heating up of the skin caused by the accumulation of body heat congest the skin, and thus lessen the amount of blood in the internal organs.

The heating pack possesses a wide range of usefulness in securing mild tonic and derivative effects.

4. ELIMINATIVE OR SWEATING WET SHEET PACK —SWEAT. W. S. P. The production of general perspiration marks the beginning of the sweating

stage. The sweating may be increased or prolonged by additional coverings, hot-water bottles placed within the folds of the dry blanket, or the drinking of hot water or lemonade at intervals. The cold compresses on the head should not be very cold nor renewed too frequently, as this depresses the thermogenic centers and prevents sweating.

Effects. The sweating wet sheet pack is a very valuable eliminative and spoliative measure. It is one of the most useful means in the treatment of the transient fevers of infants and children, in capillary bronchitis, colds, and grippe.

For spoliative purposes, it is useful in obesity and obese rheumatics.

Half Pack or Heating Trunk Pack—½ Pk.
The heating trunk pack is given in the same manner as the heating wet sheet pack, except that it includes the trunk and the hips only, the arms and the legs being excluded. A full blanket should be spread out on the treatment table, and over this placed a sheet wrung from water at 60° F., and folded to the proper width to include the trunk and the hips. The patient lies on the wet sheet, and it is drawn tightly about the body. The dry blanket is next folded over so as to bring the wet sheet in close contact with the skin surface. A moderately hot foot bath is given at the same time and continued during the treatment. The dry blanket should be laid loosely over the limbs. The pack and the patient should not be so thoroughly covered as to produce general perspiration. It is well to have a dry sheet or towels intervene between the blanket and the patient at all places not covered by the wet pack. For this purpose, a dry sheet may be spread out on the dry blanket before the wet sheet is placed for the trunk. The treatment should last about twenty or twenty-five minutes,

and be concluded with a cold mitten friction or an alternate spray douche to the parts covered by the pack and to the feet and the legs.

The effects, though less pronounced, are in general the same as those of the hot and heating trunk pack.

Hot and Heating Trunk Pack—H. & Heat. Tr. Pk. This treatment is the same as that previously described under the Winternitz coil.

A single blanket is placed crosswise of the treatment table or the bed so that the upper edge may reach well up under the arms. A sheet doubled (in case of feeble patients, a single thickness) to a width that will reach from the axillæ to below the hips is wrung from cold water and placed over the blanket. The patient lies down on this, and while both arms are raised, one end of the wet sheet is pulled tightly across and around the trunk. Over the epigastric and umbilical regions, outside of the sheet, place a three-quart hot-water bottle half filled with water at 135° F. Wrap the other end of the sheet about the trunk, over the hot-water bottle, and cover snugly with a dry blanket, folding over one end at a time. A Winternitz coil or an electric pad may be used in place of the hot-water bottle. Continue the treatment from forty minutes to two hours. General sweating should not be produced. It may be begun half an hour before the meal. Take the patient out with a cold mitten friction or an alternate spray douche to the abdomen and the spine.

Effects. The hot and heating trunk pack is the *most efficient* hydrotherapeutic measure for the treatment of *digestive disturbances.* It promotes gastric secretion and gastric digestion. Liver activity and intestinal digestion proceed more normally. Excessive peristalsis and vomiting are checked; and in decreased gastric motility, stomach movements are hastened. Because of more perfect digestion and normal peristalsis, gas formation is markedly decreased or entirely checked.

The hot and heating trunk pack is indicated in persistent vomiting, dyspepsia, flatulence, splanchnic neurasthenia, chronic congestion of the liver, and in anæmia of the liver.

In cases of almost complete arrest of gastric digestion or in persistent vomiting, the pack should be applied about twenty minutes before the meal, and continued for two or three hours. A cold mitten friction should be given at the close. The feet should be warmed by a hot foot bath before the treatment, and kept warm during the treatment. The hot foot bath may be continued while the treatment lasts, if this is not over thirty minutes; otherwise the feet should be dried and wrapped in dry flannel, so that the patient may rest more perfectly. For further details of the uses and effects, see treatment of atonic dyspepsia as given in the larger texts.

Heating Pelvic Pack—Heat. Pelv. Pk. On the treatment table, spread a blanket as for a full pack. Next fold a single blanket to form a square, and then diagonally to form a triangle. Arrange this on the large blanket so that the base is upward and the apex downward where it may be folded about the pelvis when the patient reclines. Over this, place a sheet similarly folded, and wrung nearly dry from water at 60° F, The patient then reclines, with legs flexed and knees separated, and the apex of the wet sheet is brought into close contact with the perineum and spread over the abdomen. The legs are then extended, and each lateral angle of the wet sheet is drawn tightly across the hips, the lower abdomen, and the upper thighs.

The triangular piece of dry flannel is then applied in the same manner, and the patient is covered with the large blanket. Continue the pack twenty or thirty minutes.

SPRAYS AND DOUCHES

A spray or douche consists in the projection of one or more columns of water against the body. Many different appliances are used in giving these treatments.* They possess such a wide range of adaptability that almost any desired effect may be produced by them. For this reason, the nurse should become thoroughly proficient in the use of the spray and douche controller. The water supply to the controller should come directly from hot and cold water tanks, by pipes entirely independent of all other fixtures, and no other faucets or fixtures should be attached to these mains. The most perfectly constructed controller will fail to give satisfactory results unless this rule is observed.

Shower Bath—Sh. A shower bath or rain bath consists in the projection of water in many fine streams falling upon the patient. In the shower bath, gravitation is the principal force utilized. The effect, however, is often enhanced by added pressure. The perforated disk from which the water descends should be about six inches in diameter and ten to sixteen inches above the patient's head. There should be sufficient force to cause the water to flow rapidly. The room should

---

* After many years of experience in the construction and practical use of various spray and douche controllers, a very highly efficient yet comparatively simple appliance has been evolved. It has now seen three years of experimental perfecting and practical use at the hands of the author and an experienced mechanic. So highly satisfactory has it proved, that the text here given has been revised to conform to its use; and that this may be made plainer, we have introduced an illustration, contrary to the original plan for this manual.

be very small and protected from drafts. See that the patient's feet are warm before he enters the shower. If the wetting of the hair is objectionable, as with women, protect by a rubber or mackintosh cap. Turn on the shower and adjust to the proper temperature before the patient enters.

1. HOT SHOWER—H. SH. Begin the hot shower at 100° to 105° F., and gradually raise the temperature to from 110° to 115° F., or slightly above. Time, thirty seconds to two minutes. It is used chiefly as a preparation for the cold shower or douche. A cold compress to the head may be necessary during the hot shower. If only a hot shower is prescribed, cool rapidly to 90° or 85° F., and dry quickly with sheet and towels, finishing by fanning the patient with a dry sheet.

2. COLD OR COOL SHOWER—C. SH. The cold shower is usually preceded by a hot shower. When the patient has been warmed, lower the temperature rapidly from hot to the limit of tolerance or reactive ability of the patient. Cool, 70° to 90° F. Cold, 55° to 70° F. At first, before the patient becomes accustomed to the shower, the upper limits should be utilized, and in each succeeding treatment, the temperature lowered by one or two degrees daily, and the time prolonged to from one half to three or more minutes. Effects, tonic.

3. NEUTRAL SHOWER—NEUT. SH. In giving a neutral shower, begin with the water at 100° F., and very gradually lower it to 97° to 94° F. The treatment should last from three to five minutes. The patient should be dried quickly, without percussion or unnecessary friction. Effect, sedative.

4. GRADUATED SHOWER—GRAD. SH. After a prolonged or vigorous sweating bath, it is desirable to lower the temperature of the shower slowly for

gradual cooling, and to abstract as much heat from the body as possible without producing a decided thermic reaction. Apply a cold compress to the head before the patient leaves the hot bath. Begin at 108° to 110° F., quickly raising the temperature to 115° or 118° F. Maintain this until the patient feels well warmed and is ready to welcome the cold. Gradually lower the temperature to between 80° and 90° F. Time, two to six minutes. Dry as quickly as possible with sheets and towels, and see that the patient is not exposed to cold air or drafts for at least an hour afterward.

5. REVULSIVE SHOWER—REV. SH. Begin the shower at 105° to 108° F., and gradually raise the temperature to from 110° to 115° F. or slightly above. Continue at this point for one or two minutes. When the patient has been thoroughly warmed, turn the mixer quickly to cold at a temperature of 60° to 85° F. After five to ten seconds, turn the mixer valve back to the former temperature for one or two minutes. Three complete changes from hot to cold are made. After the last cold, dry quickly with sheets and towels as usual.

Effects. The revulsive shower has a mild tonic and stimulant effect. The patient should become accustomed to it before taking the alternate hot and cold shower. The change from one to the other may be made gradually in a series of treatments by lengthening the duration of the cold with each succeeding treatment.

6. ALTERNATE HOT AND COLD SHOWER—H. & C. SH. To obtain the best results, the changes must be abrupt from hot to cold. As the water must traverse about fifteen feet of pipe before it reaches the patient, an absolutely instantaneous change is impossible. Begin with the hot at a temperature of 106° to 110° F., raising the temperature quickly

to the limit of tolerance, and continue it about one minute; then turn the mixer valve quickly to cold, and continue fifteen to thirty seconds. Reverse again to hot for about one minute, and follow this by a second cold, and so on for three complete changes of hot and cold, finishing with the cold, and drying as usual.

Effects. The alternate hot and cold shower is a vigorous tonic and stimulant. It should not be attempted without considerable preliminary training by milder measures. Some find it more agreeable than the needle spray, and easier to react to.

Sprays—Spr. A spray bath consists in the simultaneous projection of water against all parts of the body by horizontal jets surrounding the patient. For this purpose, four upright pipes, arranged in a square, and having perforations on the side of each toward the center, are used. Since these pipes are stationary, it is necessary to have a short patient stand on a stool, so that the water may not strike the face. A tall patient must bend the knees, in order to have the spray cover the entire trunk. To overcome this inconvenience, and to spread the streams of water still more, rosettes may be arranged along the pipes at intervals of sixteen inches, the upper row being movable by means of a ball joint. The effects and uses of the spray are the same as those of the shower, with the possible difference that the application is somewhat more general, and there is more or less mechanical stimulation due to percussion or pricking of the jets. This is greater as the pressure is increased by the full opening of the spray valve. Hot, cold, neutral, graduated, revulsive, and alternate treatments are given in the same manner as with the shower.

Douches—D. The douche is a local application consisting of a single or multiple column of water directed against some part of the body. It is certainly one of the most useful of all hydrotherapeutic measures. The effect of almost every other form of treatment commonly given to ambulatory patients may be approached and usually exceeded by the douche in the hands of one skilled in its application.

The necessary attachments are not numerous. These should consist of a straight nozzle; a spray nozzle, like the sprinkler of a watering pot, except that the perforated disk should have a nearly flat face; a fan douche nozzle (a movable flat piece attached to the straight nozzle will answer the same purpose); a stool with an open seat and attached upshot spray douche for administering the perineal douche.

The jet nozzle is used whenever percussion effects are desired. The pressure may be increased by opening the valve wide, or by turning into the nozzle compressed air from a separate tube. Where a percussion douche (Perc. D.) is ordered, the jet is understood. Both cold and percussion produce a decided thermic reaction, and increase the vigor and permanency of the circulatory reaction. The spray douche is useful where percussion is not desirable. The jet douche may be ''broken'' by placing the finger so as to interfere with the stream. It then resembles the spray douche in effect. The effects in general vary according to the mass, pressure, and temperature of the column of water striking the body.

The cerebral circulation will be steadied, and better general and local results obtained, if all applications of the douche begin and end with the feet. The patient should dip the hands into cold water and bathe his face before the douche is applied. In applying the douche, one should learn and systematically follow some definite plan, making changes when necessary for the particular case and condition in hand. In order to guard against burning, always keep the index finger of the hand holding the douche in contact with the stream of water as it emerges from the nozzle. This should be done with the most perfect of appliances, and even when no trouble at all is anticipated. Keep a steady hand, apply the douche accurately to the part to be treated, and have the thermometers under constant observation.

The following are the general directions for douches of different temperatures. In giving these, any form of nozzle may be used, and any portion of the body treated.

1. HOT DOUCHE—H. D. Where the hot douche alone is used, it is given for a relatively long time, two to five minutes, at a temperature of 105° to 125° F., and followed by a very brief application of cold, five to fifteen seconds, temperature 60° to 90° F. This is supposed to be just long enough to remove from the skin the heat communicated by the hot douche. The principle is identical with that of the revulsive douche, except that in the latter, three or more changes are employed, while here only one is given.

Effects. The hot douche produces dilatation of the cutaneous vessels; so where it is applied to a considerable area, effective derivation is secured. Where it is applied to a small area, the dilatation of the vessels in the deep part through a reflex channel may equal or exceed the hydrostatic effect. Percussion intensifies the reflex effect.

The hot douche is used for the relief of pain, irritation, neuralgia, sciatica, etc. In these cases, percussion is undesirable.

2. NEUTRAL DOUCHE—NEUT. D. Temperature, 94° to 97° F. Time, three to six minutes. The broken jet or spray douche is used, since sedative effects are sought. The neutral spray douche is especially beneficial when given to the spine. No force should be used, and the patient should sit on a stool, with the back to the operator. When this treatment is, given properly, the effect is that of a neutral pour.

3. COLD DOUCHE—C. D. Temperature, 55° to 70° F. The cold douche is seldom given alone; but when it is not preceded by hot, the percussion jet should be used. In this way, vigorous fluxion is produced in the part treated, with a corresponding derivation from other parts.

4. REVULSIVE DOUCHE—REV. D. Three abrupt changes from hot to cold. Temperature of the hot, 112° to 115° F. Time, thirty seconds to two minutes. Temperature of the cold, 55° to 70° F. Time, five to ten seconds. Unless this treatment is given with high pressure (percussion), the reaction is chiefly circulatory. Percussion is not usually desirable with the revulsive douche.

Effects. It will be noted that the duration of the cold is exceedingly brief as compared with the duration of the hot. In this item lies the difference between the revulsive and the alternate hot and cold douche. The effect of the revulsive douche is chiefly circulatory, and greater in the surface blood vessels than in the deep part; that is, the reflex effect is not prominent. The surface effect is that of fluxion; and if a sufficient surface is covered by the treatment, a hydrostatic (derivative) effect upon other parts is produced.

7—Hydrotherapy

The revulsive spray douche is especially applicable to the chest, the abdomen, and over the liver and the spleen, also to the spine, the pelvis, and the perineum.

5. ALTERNATE HOT AND COLD DOUCHE—H. & C. D. The method of giving the alternate douche is the same as for the revulsive douche except that the cold application is of greater duration, being from one third the duration of the hot to equal with it, so that where the hot is given for one minute, the cold should last twenty seconds to one minute, depending upon the reactive powers of the patient. Percussion (H. & C. Perc. D.) adds much to the vigor and permanency of the reaction.

Effects. The alternate hot and cold douche produces vigorous fluxion in the surface treated. When percussion is used, the reflex effects become prominent, especially if the douche is applied to only one or two parts of the body. As a general treatment, for example, the alternate hot and cold percussion douche to the spine and the legs, powerful tonic and stimulant effects are produced. The alternate percussion douche to the feet and the legs is a most efficient derivative measure, especially when preceded by the hot leg bath. The extreme fluxion it induces in the feet and the legs produces a decided and enduring derivation.

The following list of treatments, which may be given by means of the spray and douche apparatus, will help to show the technique and something of the principles involved in the effects desired.

AS A GENERAL TONIC—H. & C. Perc. D. to spine, legs, and feet.

TO PRODUCE REACTION IN ONE UNACCUSTOMED TO COLD—H. Sh. or Spr. with C. Perc. D. to spine and legs at same time.

To Relieve Congestive Headache—H. & C. Perc. D. to feet with C. Comp. to head.

Congestion of the Liver—Rev. D. (Perc. or Spr.) over hepatic area.

Sciatica—Prolonged H. D. over sciatic nerve.

Varicose Ulcers—H. & C. Spr. D. to legs, six to ten changes.

Hypochlorhydria—Rev. D. to epigastrium and H. & C. Perc. D. to mid-dorsal spine.

Lumbago—H. & C. Perc. D. to lower back.

Locomotor Ataxia and Other Flaccid Paralyses—Rev. or Alt. D. to spine.

Spastic Spinal Paralysis—Prolonged Neut. Spray D. to spine.

Chorea—Neut. D., Sh., or Spr.

Renal Congestion (Chronic)—H. & C. Perc. D. to lower third of sternum and over kidneys at back.

Chronic Pelvic Congestions—C. D. or H. & C. Perc. D. to lumbar and sacral regions.

Amenorrhea—Short C. Perc. D. to feet.

Specific Urethritis, Puritis Ani, Chronic Prostatitis, etc.—Rev. Spr. D. to perineum (called also "up spray").

Chronic Pleurisy, Unresolved Pneumonia, etc.—H. & C. Spr. D. to chest over area affected (use no force), followed by H. & C. Perc. D. to feet and legs.

Affusions. An affusion is the pouring of water from a convenient receptacle over the entire body or a portion thereof. Since the perfection of the spray and douche apparatus, the affusion has fallen into disuse in institutions equipped with such appliances. However, the pour has certain advantages that are not outweighed by the greater convenience of more complicated appliances. The flow of a considerable volume of water over a part has a somewhat different effect from a douche. Since it may be used in any home, it has a wide range of usefulness.

1. PAIL POUR OR GENERAL AFFUSION—P. P. The patient should be warm beforehand. If the treatment is given in a bathtub, he may sit; or if it is given while he is standing, the feet should be in a tub of hot water. In either case, apply a cold cephalic compress. Prepare three pails of water at different temperatures, according to the effect desired. These should be poured over the shoulders, the warmest being used first. For a mild tonic, employ pails of water at 100°, 90°, and 85° or 80° F., respectively. If the patient has just come from a warm bath of some sort, a lower temperature may be used for the first pail, and the others correspondingly lower, or only two pails used. In succeeding treatments, lower the degree of the applications until water at 50° to 60° is used for the third pail. Rub the patient vigorously after the last pail, and dry as from spray or shower. The pail pour is conveniently used after the tub or the slab shampoo, the salt glow, etc. A cold pail pour to the hips is given after the hot half bath and the hot sitz bath for revulsive effects.

2. LOCAL AFFUSIONS. These may be designated according to the part treated and the temperature of the application. A hot affusion relieves pain. The circulatory excitation soon gives way to an atonic reaction. A neutral affusion, especially to the spine, is sedative. A cold affusion, if short, is stimulating and tonic; if prolonged, it reduces congestion and inflammation, stimulating phagocytosis. A long cold pour to the head is strongly antipyretic. The alternate hot and cold pour is a powerful stimulant and tonic, producing fluxion in the part

treated, with derivation from other parts. It produces a decided local leucocytosis and stimulates phagocytosis. Because of these effects, it is a very useful measure in treating an infected part where it is impossible or undesirable to immerse the part completely in water.

In giving an affusion to the spine, have the patient sit on the edge of a bathtub or on a stool in the tub. For a pour to an arm, a hand, a foot, etc., the part may be held over a small tub while the water is poured from a pail or a large pitcher. To treat the head by a pour, have the patient lie on a cot with his head resting over the end and a tub underneath. For local affusions, the water should fall a distance of three or four inches to one or two feet, according to the part treated and the effects desired.

ENEMATA

An enema is an injection of fluid into the rectum.

GENERAL DIRECTIONS:

1. Articles Necessary. An enema can with a capacity of one half to two gallons, or a fountain syringe or a combination bag.

Five or six feet of rubber tubing with cut-off.

A glass or hard rubber enema tube.

A disinfectant solution for the enema tube. One to three per cent lysol acts both as a disinfectant and as a soap for cleansing. A water thermometer. Toilet paper.

If given in the room, there should be, in addition, a standard or hook for suspending the enema can, a bedpan, a slop jar, and several newspapers.

In the treatment room, shelves or hooks are most convenient for holding the can. They should be so arranged that the elevation of the enema can may be varied from two and one half feet to four feet above the patient.

2. Procedure. Fill the enema can with from two to six quarts of water at the proper temperature (test with a thermometer).

The patient should be warm, especially the feet. All clothing not removed should be loose.

Position of patient, dorsal, sitting, right Sims, or knee-chest.

Release the cut-off, and allow the water to run until the stream is at the same temperature as the water in the can. Close the cut-off, and lubricate the enema tube, being careful to wash it beforehand, removing the disinfectant solution.

The patient should insert the tube unless very ill or unable to do so. Instruct the patient to take as much water as possible. To make this easier, stop the flow by pinching the tube two or three times during the taking of the enema. Close the cut-off and remove the tube. If possible, the patient should retain the water a few minutes before discharging.

Repeat until a thorough bowel movement is secured or other desired result is obtained.

1. Plain Water Enemata

Rectal Injection or Enema—E. or En. In the ordinary enema, the desired amount of fluid is injected, allowed to remain a short time, and then passed. The procedure is different from rectal irrigation, in which there is a continuous inflow and outflow of fluid.

1. HOT ENEMA—H. EN. The temperature of the hot enema should vary from 103° to 110° F., according to the condition of the patient and the

result desired. It is useful in relieving irritation, the pain of inflammation in the rectum or prostate, and pain of hemorrhoids. It also aids in expelling gas, and helps to check diarrhea by decreasing rectal tenesmus. It may be used as a preliminary measure in the treatment of dysmenorrhea. The hot enema is also used to warm and stimulate the body in shock.

2. WARM ENEMA—EN. The ordinary enema for cleansing purposes should be given at a temperature of 95° to 100° F. Where it has to be repeated frequently, use tepid water, that is, 80° to 92° F., to avoid, as far as possible, the relaxing effect of warm water.

3. COLD ENEMA—C. EN. For the cool or cold enema, the temperature of the water may vary from 55° to 80° F. Up to about 70° F., it may be regarded as cold; and from 70° to 80° F., as cool. The cold enema is a powerful stimulant to bowel movements, and should be more generally used for this purpose in place of the warm enema. For this reason, it is useful in overcoming the enema and cathartic habits. If retained ten or fifteen minutes or frequently repeated, it is useful in shrinking hemorrhoids. It may also be used in fever; but for this purpose, prolonged rectal irrigation is much more convenient and effective.

Graduated Enema—Grad. E. The graduated enema is not a single treatment, but a series of treatments. It is used to overcome the enema and cathartic habits. As usually given, it extends over a period of ten to twelve days. It should be preceded by thorough coloclysters of water at 90° tó 100° F., to remove accumulated feces.

The series of enemata is begun with a large

amount of tepid water, and finished with a small amount of cold water, one enema being given daily.

First day	- -	4½ pints	at 94° F.
Second day	- -	4 pints	at 90° F.
Third day	- -	3½ pints	at 86° F.
Fourth day	- -	3 pints	at 82° F.
Fifth day	- -	2½ pints	at 78° F.
Sixth day	- -	2 pints	at 74° F.
Seventh day	- -	1½ pints	at 70° F.
Eighth day	- -	1 pint	at 66° F.
Ninth day	- -	½ pint	at 62° F.
Tenth day	- -	¼ pint	at 58° F.

The above program is suggestive only; the variations in the amount and temperature of the water should be made to suit the needs of the case. The entire series, with the exception of the temperatures above 80° F., may need to be repeated. Cold enemata should not be given during the menses.

Effects. After prolonged use of cathartics, the muscular part of the intestinal wall becomes relaxed and atonic because of overstimulation. The response to drug and chemical excitants is worn out, and it is necessary that the atony be overcome by some more physiologic means. Repeated use of the warm or hot enema also causes relaxation, with stretching and distension of the wall of the rectum and of the lower sigmoid flexure.

The contact with the cold water introduced into the bowel is an effective means of combating this atony and distension. By the gradual reduction in the temperature, a response can be brought about even after the atony has existed for some time. Both this treatment and alternate hot and cold rectal irrigation are very efficient in cases of atonic constipation. They may be advantageously combined with the use of slow intrarectal and abdominal sinusoidal electricity, abdominal massage, vibration, and spinal nerve stimulation.

Rectal Irrigation—Rec. Irrig. In giving rectal irrigation, a special tube is used, which is provided with an inlet and a return flow, so that the fluid passes into the rectum, bathing the mucous membrane, and returns through the outlet. These are made of hard rubber or metal. The patient should be in the dorsal or the Sims position. The enema can should be eighteen inches or two feet above the patient. A piece of rubber tubing should be attached to the outflow tube, so as to carry the outflow into the toilet fixture, or, if given to a bed patient, into a jar placed at the side of the bed.

1. HOT RECTAL IRRIGATION—H. REC. IRRIG. When the water used is at a temperature of 102° to 105° or 106° F., the treatment produces decided effects in the relief of pain and rectal tenesmus. It may also be used with great benefit in cases of chronic cystitis with frequent and painful urination.

2. COLD RECTAL IRRIGATION—C. REC. IRRIG. Cold rectal irrigation is a very useful antipyretic measure. For this purpose, the water should not be very cold, but from about 70° to 80° F., and the treatment should be continued about forty-five minutes at a time.

Cold irrigation is also useful in stimulating bowel movement; but for this purpose, it possesses no advantage over the cold enema.

3. ALTERNATE HOT AND COLD RECTAL IRRIGATION —ALT. H. & C. REC. IRRIG. In giving alternate hot and cold irrigation, it is necessary to use two enema cans, with tubing connected by a Y tube, so that the alternations may be controlled. The hot should be allowed to run from one half to two minutes, and the cold from fifteen to thirty seconds. From

five to twelve or more complete changes may be made in a single treatment. The greater the extremes of temperature, the greater will be the effect. It is possible to use a plain enema tube, injecting but a small amount, and allowing the water to pass out through the enema tube after each injection.

This treatment is a most efficient measure in the relief of chronic inflammations of the pelvic organs, especially of the bladder, the prostate, the posterior urethra, and the rectum. It is also one of the most effective means of combating chronic atonic constipation.

Coloclyster—Ccl. In a coloclyster, the fluid is introduced into the colon. When the coloclyster is used to produce thorough cleansing of the large bowel, four to six pints of water or saline solution at a temperature of 100° to 104° F. are used for each injection. An ordinary enema, and if necessary, a soapsuds enema, is first used to cleanse the lower bowel. The patient takes the knee-chest or the right Sims position. Use an ordinary enema tube; but if results are not obtained, it may be necessary to use the high bowel catheter (colon tube). As the water enters, rub along the colon up the left side, across the abdomen, and down on the right side, so as to fill the large bowel well. As much water as possible should be injected, but this should be done slowly. Remove the enema or colon tube, and as the water is expelled, reverse the movements along the colon to favor complete emptying. It may be necessary to repeat the procedure.

Effects. The coloclyster is used to produce a full, complete evacuation of the bowels, and for cleansing the large bowel in cases where an ordinary enema does not produce the desired results. It is also used to remove fecal impaction. When some medicament or antiseptic is introduced, it may be used to disinfect the large intestine or to destroy parasites. (See "Quassia Enema.")

2. Medicated Enemata

Saline Enema—Sal. En. For whatever purpose the saline enema is used, it should be preceded by a thorough cleansing enema, unless the bowel has already been cleared of feces.

1. SALINE ENEMA TO BE RETAINED AND ABSORBED. The absorption of saline fluid from the rectum is useful in hemorrhage, surgical shock, and pelvic and abdominal abscesses after drainage has been instituted. To be absorbed most rapidly, the sodium chloride solution should be isotonic with blood serum, or slightly hypotonic. A physiologic salt solution is so called because it is isotonic with blood serum.

Intermittent Proctoclysis. One half pint of physiologic salt solution (0.95 per cent) at a temperature of 100° to 105° F. is given slowly or by high bowel catheter. To make this, use one level teaspoonful (4.5 grams or less) to the pint of water. For a hypotonic solution (more rapid absorption), use a little less salt. After this has been absorbed, another one half pint may be given. If this amount is not readily retained, use four or five ounces only.

Continuous Proctoclysis. The method first introduced by Murphy has undergone considerable change in technique, but is still known as the Murphy drip, or the drop method. It has become a routine procedure after many major operations, especially those involving hemorrhage or shock, and is continued until the patient is able to take and retain sufficient fluid by mouth. A two-quart container should be suspended about two or three feet above the bed, and the outflow through the dropping bulb controlled by a screw cut-off. The saline solution is given just fast enough to allow of its absorption by the large bowel. This will be about one and one half to two pints in forty to sixty minutes; and the rate of flow, about sixty drops a minute. This may be repeated every two hours, or as conditions require.

The rectal tube should be a small size bowel catheter of rather resistant rubber, so that it will not be readily kinked or compressed. Hard rubber or glass tubes are unsatisfactory. A hot-water bottle may be placed on the bed, over the rubber tubing, to maintain the proper temperature of the solution.

For the acidosis of diabetes, various infectious and other metabolic diseases, an alkaline solution should be given by Murphy drip. Several different formulas are employed for this purpose. One very widely used consists of one dram of sodium bicarbonate and one ounce of glucose to each pint of water. For stimulation, a decoction of coffee may be administered by protoclysis. In case of operations on jaundiced persons, a weak solution of calcium chloride may be used by rectum after operation, as well as being administered by mouth before. It greatly lessens the danger of hemorrhage.

2. SALINE ENEMA TO CAUSE EXOSMOSIS, acting like a saline cathartic. Used to produce exosmosis, the enema is designed for thorough cleansing of the mucous membrane, and is of inestimable value in chronic mucous colitis.

To produce exosmosis (that is, to draw water from the tissues into the bowel), the solution must be hypertonic—of greater concentration than blood serum. Three pints of warm or hot water is used, containing about two teaspoonfuls of salt or one fourth teaspoonful of Epsom salts added to a physiologic salt solution. The enema should be introduced into the colon by a high bowel catheter, or its flow into the colon aided by the knee-chest position. Let it be retained fifteen to twenty minutes or longer. If retained much over half an hour, some fluid will be absorbed. The treatment should always be preceded by an ordinary enema to remove feces.

Mayo Gas Enema. After abdominal and pelvic operations, this solution is very beneficial to remove accumulated gas in the intestines. It may be given a pint or more at a time and repeated as necessary. To each pint of water, add two drams of sodium bicarbonate and one ounce of glucose.

Soapsuds Enema—S. S. En. Prepare two or three pints of warm soapsuds solution, made by scraping Castile or Ivory soap and mixing thoroughly in water at about 100° F. Follow by a plain enema to remove the soapsuds.

Effects. The soapsuds enema facilitates evacuation of the bowels, and should be used where the plain enema fails to produce results.

Oil Enema—Oil En. In administering the oil enema, use the colon tube with a small enema can, giving one and one half to three or four ounces of warmed cottonseed or other vegetable oil. It should be retained from two to ten or twelve hours or overnight. Pass it the next morning, and follow by soapsuds and plain enemata.

Effects. The oil enema is used to remove hardened or impacted feces. It has a soothing, relaxing effect, and is therefore used to overcome spastic constipation, as of chronic lead poisoning.

When given two or three days after an operation for hemorrhoids, it softens and loosens the clot, so that it passes without causing pain or starting fresh bleeding.

Honey or Molasses Enema. Give one half to one pint of warmed molasses solution, consisting of two parts soapsuds and one of molasses, by high bowel catheter. Follow by plain enema.

Effects. The honey or molasses enema has a purging effect similar to that of the hypertonic saline enema. It aids in removing the mucous casts and mucous accumulations of chronic colitis, and is also useful as a gas enema.

Asafetida Enema. To one pint of warm water, add four ounces of an emulsion of asafetida, prepared by agitating one half dram of asafetida powder in four ounces of water; or add one ounce of tincture of asafetida to a pint of warm water. Give as an ordinary enema. It is used to expel flatus.

Turpentine Enema. To a pint of soapsuds solution add ten to twenty drops of oil of turpentine. Follow by a plain enema. The turpentine enema is given in the same way and for the same purpose as the asafetida enema. Its action is somewhat more vigorous. It should not be used where there is kidney irritation or Bright's disease.

Glycerin and Epsom Salts Enema. The glycerin and Epsom salts enema is a vigorous purgative. It is used in cases of fecal impaction and obstinate constipation (obstipation).

Just before using, prepare a mixture consisting of two ounces of magnesium sulphate, two ounces of glycerin, and sufficient warm water (about two ounces) to make it pass readily through the colon tube.

First cleanse the lower bowel from feces, and then inject the mixture by high bowel catheter, using gentle pressure with a rubber bulb if necessary. Considerable patience and persistence may be necessary to secure results.

Starch Enema. The warm starch enema is given to relieve irritation and check diarrhea. Make a thin paste of starch in one or two ounces of cold water. Add hot water enough to make from four ounces to one pint of solution. Inject slowly after giving a hot cleansing enema. The sedative effect may be made greater and pain relieved by adding five to twenty drops of laudanum.

Astringent Enema. An astringent mixture is useful in controlling or checking diarrhea and dysentery; also in inflammation of the rectum. The bowel should be cleansed by a plain enema of warm or hot water before the astringent is injected. Usually from four to eight ounces is all that is desirable. Either of the following formulas may be used:

a. A heaping tablespoon of tannin to one pint of water at 100° F.

b. An ounce of glycerite of tannin to one pint of water at 100° F.

Quassia Enema. The quassia enema is used to destroy and remove threadworms, or pinworms (oxyuris vermicularis). Prepare an infusion of quassia by pouring over one and one half drams of finely rasped quassia wood, twenty ounces of warm water; let it stand twenty to thirty minutes, and strain. Use a plain cleansing enema first; then cleanse the colon thoroughly with warm water containing a teaspoonful of borax to the pint. Now inject into the colon (coloclyster) a half pint to a pint of the infusion of quassia; retain as long as possible. A 1 to 10,000 bichloride solution may be used instead of the quassia. It should not be retained very long.

VAGINAL DOUCHES AND IRRIGATION

A vaginal douche consists in the flushing or irrigating of the vaginal cavity by a fluid.

GENERAL DIRECTIONS:

1. Articles Necessary in the Treatment Room. Douche table, fountain syringe or douche can with a capacity of one or two gallons, five or six feet of rubber tubing, douche tube of glass or hard rubber, lubricant, disinfectant, sheets, and napkins. Additional need in private room, standard or hooks for douche can, a douche pan, slop jar, and rubber sheeting or paper.

2. Procedure. Preparation of the douche: Fill the can with from two to four quarts of water at the prescribed temperature, and place it from three to four feet above the patient. Always use a thermometer in preparing vaginal douches.

Preparation of patient: If the clothing is not removed, protect thoroughly. Always cover the patient with a sheet. Lubricate the tube with vaseline or soap. Release the cut-off, and allow the water to run a few seconds. Instruct the patient to insert the tube, unless she is helpless.

Position of patient, dorsal, with hips raised, and thighs and legs flexed.

1. Plain Vaginal Irrigation

Vaginal Irrigation for Ordinary Use. 1. HOT VAGINAL IRRIGATION—V. I. This is used for cleansing purposes. Two to four quarts of water is employed, at a temperature of 105° to 115° F. Finish with a pint of water at 70° F.

In the treatment of pelvic inflammations, the hot vaginal douche is usually given as a preliminary to the use of the hot sitz bath, the hot half bath, or the hip-and-leg pack.

2. VERY HOT VAGINAL IRRIGATION—H. V. ,I. The very hot vaginal irrigation is designed for the relief of pain or to check hemorrhage. Two to four quarts of water is used, at a temperature of 110° to 125° F.

3. ALTERNATE HOT AND COLD VAGINAL IRRIGA-TION—H. & C. V. I. Alternate hot and cold vaginal irrigation is given for tonic and stimulating effects. It is also useful in chronic pelvic inflammations. Use two cans with a Y tube connection. Put four quarts of water in one can, at a temperature of 110° to 120° F.; and two quarts of water in the other, at a temperature of 70° F.

Give the hot fifteen to twenty seconds, and the cold five to ten seconds. Continue the alternations for five to ten minutes, beginning with hot and finishing with cold.

Vaginal Irrigation During Pregnancy. During pregnancy, certain precautions must be observed. The pressure of the water must not be too great; that is, the douche can must not be placed too high. Very cold water or extremely hot water should not be used. It is positively necessary that the openings in the bulb of the douche tube be lateral and not directly on the end. During pregnancy, vaginal irrigation is given chiefly for cleansing, for the treatment of leucorrhea, and for the relief of irritation. Use two to four quarts of water, at a temperature of 98° to 105° F. Hang the douche can twelve to eighteen inches above the hips.

2. Disinfectant and Medicated Douches

Soapsuds Vaginal Irrigation—S. S. V. I.
Use two quarts of soapsuds solution prepared from laundry soap or green soap solution, at a temperature of 105° to 110° F. Wrap the tube in cheesecloth, and swab the vagina carefully, but thoroughly, while the water is flowing. Follow by plain vaginal irrigation, then give a permanganate or bichloride douche.

The soapsuds vaginal irrigation is used to prepare patients for surgical operations, or for special cleansing and disinfectant purposes.

Permanganate of Potassium Vaginal Irrigation—P. V. I. To one quart of water add two drams (two teaspoonfuls) of a saturated solution of potassium permanganate—(1 to 2,000). Temperature, 110° to 120° F. Precede by a plain vaginal irrigation. Oxalic acid (sat. sol.) will remove the stain.

The permanganate douche is used as a deodorant and a disinfectant in the treatment of vaginal inflammations, leucorrhea, etc., also as a disinfectant preparatory to operation.

Bichloride of Mercury Vaginal Irrigation—Bichlor. V. I. Use one dram (a teaspoonful) of a saturated solution of bichloride of mercury to one or two quarts of water (1 to 4,000 or 8,000). Temperature, 110° to 115° F.

Always precede by a plain vaginal irrigation, so as to remove all mucus and other secretions. If this is not done, the disinfectant properties of the bichloride are lessened by its combination with albuminous substances.

Carbolic Acid Vaginal Irrigation—Carb. V. I. Use one half ounce of a five per cent solu-

tion to one quart of water. Temperature, 110°
to 115° F.

Be sure that the solution is thoroughly mixed
with the water, otherwise a carbolic acid burn may
result. Always have alcohol at hand in giving
this douche.

Creolin or Lysol Vaginal Irrigation. Use
a one-per-cent or a two-per-cent solution of either
lysol or creolin in water at a temperature of 110°
to 120° F. These disinfectants are much used
after confinement where puerperal infection has oc-
curred, or in case of a suspicious odor to the lochia.

Acetic Acid or Vinegar Vaginal Irrigation.
The acetic acid douche is used to check hemorrhage. Use one quart of boiled vinegar to one
quart of water, or one ounce of glacial acetic acid
to one quart of water. Temperature, 115° to 120° F.

Alum Vaginal Irrigation—Alum V. I. The
alum douche is also used to check hemorrhage or
prolonged menses. Add one pint of a saturate
solution of alum to one pint of water. Temperature, 115° to 120° F. Precede by a plain hot vaginal irrigation.

Swedish Massage

1. GENERAL

Arms.

1. Lubricate from wrist to shoulder twice, coming down to hand with four rotary sweeps.

2. Friction from hand to shoulder.

3. Fulling from shoulder to hand, once.

4. Spiral friction from hand to shoulder, twice
to each side of arm, beginning on the inside of
the arm.

5. Pétrissage from the hand to the elbow three times, friction. Repeat pétrissage and friction; rotary kneading to elbow. Treat arm same as forearm.

6. Rolling, down three times, alternating with upward friction.

7. Friction from hand to shoulder.

8. Wringing from shoulder to hand, once.

9. Friction from hand to shoulder.

10. Percussion from shoulder to hand; hacking, spatting, beating, down and up each side, once.

11. Joint movements—flexion and extension; circumduction.

12. Vibration and stroking.

Chest.

1. Lubricate.

2. Friction.

3. Fulling down one side and up the other.

4. Friction.

5. Palm kneading, twice, beginning on neck; second time, omitting neck.

6. Friction.

7. Percussion with deep breathing; tapping, hacking, spatting.

8. Stroking.

Legs.

1. Lubricate.

2. Friction up.

3. Fulling down.

4. Spiral friction up, twice to each side of leg, beginning on inside.

5. Friction up, circular and centripetal.

6. Pétrissage:

   a. Foot.

   b. Leg to knee, three times, alternating with friction. Repeat.

c. Rotary to knee.

d. Thigh same as leg.

7. Rolling down three times, alternating with upward friction.

8. Friction up.

9. Wringing down.

10. Friction up.

11. Percussion, down and up each side, once; hacking, spatting, beating; clapping to thigh only.

12. Joint movements—flexion and extension; circumduction.

13. Vibration and stroking.

Abdomen.

1. Lubricate.
2. Deep breathing.
3. Inspiratory lifting.
4. Lifting of abdominal viscera.
5. Reflex stroking.
6. Deep vibration.
7. Lateral and circular shaking.
8. Percussion; tapping, hacking, spatting, and beating; clapping to colon.
9. Fist kneading to colon, twice.
10. Friction.
11. Fulling down and up recti muscles, to and from the median line, down on one side and up on the other.
12. Pétrissage to recti muscles, twice to each side, alternating with friction.
13. Stroking.

Hips.

1. Lubricate.
2. Friction.
3. Fulling down and up each side.
4. Circular friction, twice.

5. Pétrissage to each side, twice, alternating with friction.
6. Palm kneading, twice.
7. Friction, light centripetal.
8. Percussion; hacking, spatting, beating, and clapping.
9. Stroking.

Back.

1. Lubricate.
2. Friction.
3. Fulling down one side and up the other.
4. Friction.
5. Thumb kneading to spine.
6. Pétrissage, twice to each side, alternating with friction.
7. Circular digital kneading down each side of spine (reënforced).
8. Digital friction down spine, twice (reënforced).
9. Palm kneading to shoulders, digital kneading to ribs.
10. Palm kneading down each side of spine (reënforced).
11. Muscle grasping, down and up spine.
12. Digital kneading down spine.
13. Heavy transverse wringing, up and down.
14. Percussion; hacking, spatting, beating, and clapping.
15. Stroking, covering entire back; digital stroking to ribs. Finish with six light friction strokes to spine.

2. SPECIAL

Massage to Abdomen for Constipation.

1. Lubricate.
2. Deep breathing.

3. Inspiratory lifting.
4. Lifting of abdominal viscera.
5. Reflex stroking.
6. Deep vibration.
7. Lateral and circular shaking.
8. Percussion to colon; tapping, hacking, spatting, beating, and clapping.
9. Digital kneading to colon, four times.
10. Fist kneading to colon, four times.
11. Kneading of colon with heel of hand and fingers.
12. Friction.
13. Mass kneading.
14. Rolling.
15. Fulling.
16. Friction.
17. Pétrissage as in general massage.
18. Percussion to lumbar spine.
19. Exercise, hips raising with legs closing and parting with deep breathing.

Massage for Sprained Ankle.

1. Lubricate.
2. Friction up to above knee, beginning at foot.
3. Fulling down.
4. Spiral friction to each side, beginning on inside of leg.
5. Pétrissage the same as in general massage, beginning near knee and working toward the ankle as the patient can bear it. Avoid hurting patient.
6. Stroking up.
7. Rotary kneading to knee for five minutes.
8. Stroke leg upward.
9. Digital kneading to foot for five minutes. Give carefully.
10. Stroke leg upward.

11. Pétrissage, alternating with friction or stroking.

12. Wring down if patient can stand it.

13. Stroke upward. Elevate foot and ankle by putting something underneath.

Massage to Head.

1. Friction from edge of hair to crown of head.
2. Stroking.
3. Digital kneading from edge of hair to crown of head.
4. Stroking.
5. Chucking.
6. Stroking.
7. Circular digital kneading.
8. Stroking.
9. Repeat all movements.
10. Percussion; tapping, hacking.
11. Head movements: back, forth, bending with resistance; circumduction.

Massage to Face.

1. Friction to face and neck.
2. Fulling, down one side and up the other, avoiding the forehead.
3. Stroking.
4. Digital kneading, down and up each side, beginning at middle of forehead.
5. Special attention to eye, nose, mouth, and wrinkles.
6. Stroking.
7. Pétrissage, down one side and up the other.
8. Special attention to eye, nose, mouth, and wrinkles.
9. Stroking.
10. Circular digital kneading down and up each side.

11. Special attention to eye, nose, mouth, and wrinkles.

12. Stroking.

13. Palm kneading.

14. Special attention to eye, nose, mouth, and wrinkles.

15. Cheek twisting.

16. Special attention to eye, nose, mouth, and wrinkles.

17. Percussion; tapping, hacking.

18. Head movements: back and forth, bending with resistance; circumduction.

19. Vibration, nose and sides of head.

20. Stroking.

Index of Abbreviations in Common Use in Prescription Writing

Abd .... Abdomen
Alc. R. .... Alcohol rub
Alk. B. .... Alkaline bath
Alk. Spg. .... Alkaline sponge

B. .... Bath

C. B. or C. Tub ..... Cold tub bath
Ccl. .... Coloclyster
C. Coil .... Cold water coil
C. Comp. .... Cold compress
C. En. .... Cold enema
C. F. or Cf. or Cpr. . Centripetal friction
C. Ft. B. .... Shallow cold foot bath
Ch. .... Chest
Ch. Pk. .... Moist chest pack
C. M. F. or Cmf. .... Cold mitten friction
C. Rec. Irrig. .... Cold rectal irrigation
C. Rub. B. .... Cold rubbing bath
C. Rub. Z. .... Cold rubbing sitz
C. S. B. .... Cold shallow bath
C. Sh. .... Cold shower
C. Spg. .... Cold sponging
C. T. R. or Ctr. ..... Cold towel rub
C. Z. .... Cold sitz

D. .... Douche (not vaginal irrigation)
D. B. P. .... Dry blanket pack
D. F. .... Dry friction or dry rub

Dhr. .... Dry hand friction or rub
Drip. Sh. R. .... Dripping sheet rub

E. or En. .... Enema
Eff. B. .... Effervescent or Nauheim bath
E. L. B. .... Electric light bath
Elec. Pk. .... Electrothermal pack
Evap. W. S. P. ..... Evaporating wet sheet pack

Fo. .... Fomentations
Ft. B. .... Foot bath

Grad. B. .... Graduated bath
Grad. En. .... Graduated enema
Grad. Sh. .... Graduated shower

H. & C. D. .... Hot and cold douche
H. & C. Ft. B. ..... Alternate hot and cold foot bath
H. & C. Hd. .... Alternate hot and cold to head
H. & C. Lg. B. ..... Alternate hot and cold leg bath
H. & C. Rec. Irrig. . Hot and cold rectal irrigation
H. & C. Sh. .... Hot and cold shower
H. & C. Sp. .... Hot and cold to spine
H. & C. V. I. ...... Hot and cold vaginal irrigation
H. B. or H. Tub .... Hot tub bath
H. B. P. .... Full hot blanket pack
H. Comp. .... Hot gauze compress
H. & Heat. Tr. Pk. .. Hot and heating trunk pack
H. D. .... Hot douche
Heat. Pelv. Pk. ..... Heating pelvic pack
Heat. Th. Comp. ..... Heating compress to throat
Heat. W. S. P. ..... Heating wet sheet pack
H. En. .... Hot enema
H. Ft. B. .... Hot foot bath
H. Hp. & Lg. Pk. ... Hot hip-and-leg pack
H. Lg. B. .... Hot leg bath
H. Lg. Pk. .... Hot leg pack
H. Pelv. Pk. .... Hot pelvic pack
H. Rec. Irrig. ...... Hot rectal irrigation
H. Sh. .... Hot shower
H. Spg. .... Hot sponging
H. Tr. Pk. .... Hot trunk pack
H. Tub or H. B. .... Hot tub bath
H. V. I. .... Very hot vaginal irrigation
H. ½ B. .... Hot half bath
½ Pk. .... Heating trunk pack or half pack

Ice Bg. .... Ice bag
Ice Pk. .... Ice pack

Lg. B. .... Leg bath

M. A. B. .... Moist abdominal bandage or girdle
Menth. R. .... Menthol rub
Mss. .... General massage
Mss. Abd. .... Abdominal massage

Neut. B. .... Neutral bath

Neut. D. .... Neutral douche
Neut. Farad. .... Neutral faradic bath
Neut. Galv. .... Neutral galvanic bath
Neut. Sh. .... Neutral shower
Neut. Sinu. .... Neutral sinusoidal bath
Neut. W. S. P. ..... Neutral wet sheet pack
Néut. Z. .... Neutral sitz bath
Nk. .... Neck

O² B. .... Oxygen bath
Oil En. .... Oil enema
O. R. .... Oil rub

Perc. D. .... Percussion douche
P. P. .... Pail pour
P. V. I. .... Potassium permanganate vaginal
                         irrigation
Rad. Héat. .... Radiant heat
R. Ch. Pk. .... Roller chest pack
Rec. Irrig. .... Rectal irrigation
Rev. Comp. .... Revulsive compress
Rev. D. .... Revulsive douche
Rev. Pelv. Pk. ..... Revulsive pelvic pack
Rev. Tr. Pk. .... Revulsive trunk pack
Rev. Z. .... Revulsive sitz
Russ. B. .... Russian bath

Sal. B. .... Saline bath
Sal. En. .... Saline enema
Sal. Spg. .... Saline sponge
Sgl. .... Salt glow or salt rub
Sh. .... Shower
Simul. H. & C. Hd. .. Simultaneous hot and cold to head
Sp. .... Spine
Spg. .... Sponging
Spr. .... Spray bath
Spr. D. .... Spray douche
Sq. Ch. Pk. .... Square chest pack
S. S. En. .... Soapsuds enema
Ssh. .... Swedish shampoo
S. S. V. I. .... Soapsuds vaginal irrigation
St. .... Stomach
Sweat. W. S. P. .... Sweating wet sheet pack

Talc. R. .... Talcum rub
Tub Sh. .... Tub shampoo
Tur. B. .... Turkish bath
Tur. Sh. .... Turkish shampoo

Up Spr. .... Up spray or spray douche to
                         perineum

V. I. .... Vaginal irrigation

W. H. R. or Whr. ... Wet hand rub
W. Sh. R. .... Wet sheet rub
W. S. P. .... Full wet sheet pack
Wzr. .... Witch-hazel rub

Z. .... Sitz bath

INDEX